Everyday Home Repairs

Contents

The Tools

For any kind of maintenance work about the house you are going to need a selection of tools. How many you require and what type of tool is often a difficult question—there are hundreds to choose from and with such a selection it is easy to buy tools that you will hardly ever use. But, of course, when you do need them they are often indispensable. I have selected a basic kit which should cover most emergencies about the house :

Hammer

Hammers are the most common tools in use and there are several different types : peine, ball peine and claw. These are available in different head weights. I would suggest a claw hammer of 566g (20oz) weight as this will not only put nails in, but also pull them out should you bend one, thus doing two jobs for the price of one.

Maintenance

Keep the face of the hammer clean and free from glue, paint and grease (*see* 'Nails' for the reasons why, p 6).

Saw

When choosing a saw look for one with a handle which does not cramp the hand, and make sure that it balances well. Some saws have a 90° × 45° angle formed in the handle which acts as a square for setting out the timber to be cut and saves money on buying a separate square. Seven teeth per 25mm (1in) is a good saw to begin with. If you choose a hard point, that is, with the teeth specially hardened at

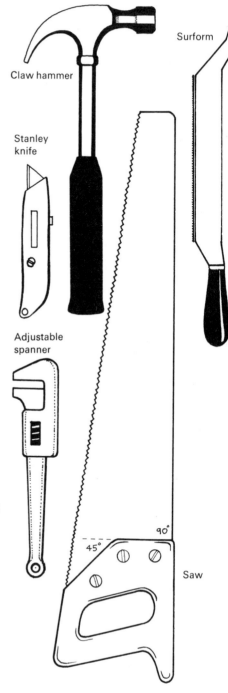

Claw hammer

Surform

Stanley knife

Adjustable spanner

Saw

2

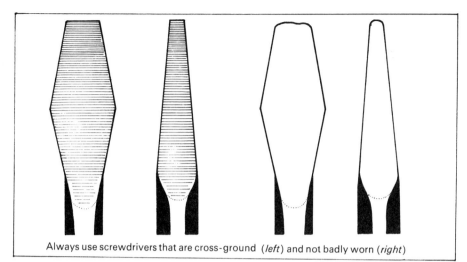

Always use screwdrivers that are cross-ground (*left*) and not badly worn (*right*)

the factory, the saw will stay sharp for a long time ; however this type of saw cannot be resharpened like a conventional one. With care and if not used every day it will last a very long time.

If you use a conventional saw it is a very skilful job to set and sharpen it, but there are now devices on the market to make this job easier for the amateur. You will have to decide which type to buy, but do remember that a blunt saw or a saw without enough set on will not cut square or true. You will have to use much more pressure to make it work and thus increase the risk of it slipping and giving you a cut hand.

Maintenance

Lightly oil after use.

Screwdriver

When selecting a screwdriver look first at the handle to make sure it affords a good purchase and is comfortable in the hand. The blade should be cross ground for maximum strength. Choose three different sizes, small, medium and large. These will manage most of your maintenance jobs and the selection can be added to later.

Maintenance

Keep the ends of the screwdriver ground flat. Unless you have a grindstone this will have to be done at your local garage. Badly worn screwdrivers soil the end of the screw and make it very difficult to drive in.

Note Screwdrivers should never be used for lifting floorboards, removing skirting boards, cutting holes in cement or for general prising.

The three tools just described are the essentials. Useful additions are : a surform ; an adjustable spanner ; a Stanley knife ; and an electric or hand drill. Remember when buying always to choose good quality tools, and never be tempted to save money by buying cheap, inferior ones. Look after them with care and they will last a lifetime.

Materials

Timber

To do any job around the house you will need materials of some sort whether it be nails, screws, timber or whatever. Let us turn first to the developments in timber.

Wood comes in all sizes and shapes, in both soft and hardwood. DIY shops, builders' merchants and timber importers are the source of supply.

Sawn timber generally comes in the size stated, ie 25×25mm (1×1in) but if the wood is planed (abbreviated PAR—'planed all round') then it will finish approximately 22×22mm ($\frac{7}{8} \times \frac{7}{8}$in). It is as well to allow for these differences if you are working on a project.

Softwood is the wood most commonly available. Select your own lengths, and look for straight, dry and true timber, avoiding dead knots, shakes, twists and splits. Most timber

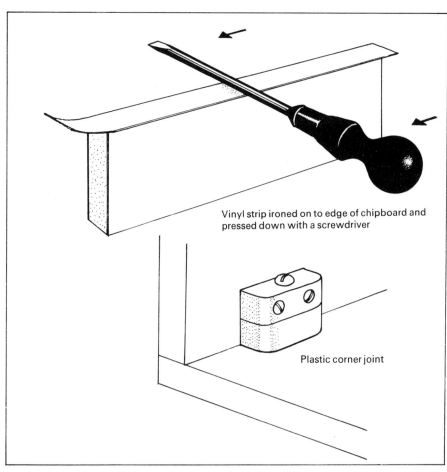

Vinyl strip ironed on to edge of chipboard and pressed down with a screwdriver

Plastic corner joint

merchants will cut timber off to the length required so measure the job in hand before you set off to buy the timber.

Plywood consists of a number of layers of thin veneer glued together, giving immense strength and used for a wide variety of working jobs. The standard sizes are as follows : 3mm, 4mm, 6mm and 12mm ($\frac{1}{8}$in, $\frac{1}{6}$in, $\frac{1}{4}$in and $\frac{1}{2}$in).

Blockboard is similar to plywood, having thin veneers of plywood stuck to a core made from strips of softwood and as the sizes are generally thicker than plywood, 18mm and 25mm ($\frac{3}{4}$in and 1in), it is ideal for use in large areas.

Chipboard is manufactured from small chippings of wood, hence the name. The chippings are bonded with adhesive and then pressed to the required thickness. This material is ideal for roof cladding, though some other uses include furniture that is to be covered with fabric, doors and vertical partitions. Do not use it for shelves as chipboard will sag under its own weight. Standard sizes are 12mm and 18mm ($\frac{1}{2}$in and $\frac{3}{4}$in).

A recent development in chipboard is to cover the face of it with either a wood veneer, melamine or with a vinyl face. This type of material is often used by kitchen-unit manufacturers. Known as 'faced boards' these have meant big gains for the DIY person, due to the vast number of sizes available. Several different wood veneers are available, oak, mahogany, teak, etc, which can be polished to match any existing furniture. Matching edging-strips of wood and vinyl are also available.

These strips are easy to fix : you simply use a domestic iron as the edging strips are coated on the back with a hot melt glue. Place the cut strip on the edge to be covered then, using a piece of brown paper to protect the face of the wood or vinyl, just rub the iron along the strip until the glue melts and sticks to the edge of the board. Next, press the strip down with a screwdriver to compress the edges, then wait to allow the glue to harden. After one hour rub the edges flush with a fine grade sandpaper.

Cutting these boards calls for a sharp saw and always score a line with a knife on both sides of the board as this will stop the veneer tearing as you cut, and will also leave a clean edge for sticking on the edging strip. One disadvantage with this type of board is that unless well supported it is unsuitable for shelves due to the chipboard core. Chipboard is most suitable for building any type of furniture and requires little or no skill since you only need the ability to cut the board to the required length and to use a domestic iron. Simple plastic corner-blocks will make a firm secure joint. Standard lengths are : 1.8m (6ft) and 2.4m (8ft) ; standard widths are : 150mm (6in), 225mm (9in), 300mm (12in), 375mm (15in), 450mm (18in), 525mm (21in), 600mm (24in), 675mm (27in) and 750mm (30in).

Hardboard is used for all manner of things : cladding for partitions, backs of cupboards, levelling old floorboards, pelmets, etc. When using hardboard make sure that there are enough supports, as this material tends to sag in the same manner as chipboard.

Materials

Nails

There are many different sorts of nail, but I shall deal only with those most widely used about the home. Before discussing them in detail, it is worth making the point that nails will bend if not driven in properly, and this can be avoided by always making sure that the face of the hammer is clean. New hammers are coated with sealer to prevent rust while in storage before being sold, and so the first job with a new hammer is to rub the face on a piece of fine sandpaper to remove this film of lacquer.

When using glue or any substitute that will adhere to the face of the hammer, the same procedure applies—always clean it off.

The smallest nail in general use is the panel pin. This is available in sizes ranging from less than 12mm ($\frac{1}{2}$in) to 50mm (2in) and is used for thin sheet material such as hardboard and plywood. Up to about 12mm ($\frac{1}{2}$in) panel pins are ideally suited for framing pictures since they have a very small head and are unlikely to split the wood. Some lengths are available with a diamond head (see drawing), and once driven home these need no punching in to hide this head as with the conventional panel pin.

Oval nails are perhaps the most common and are used in all types of work. Sizes vary from 22mm ($\frac{7}{8}$in) to 65mm ($2\frac{3}{4}$in). Their main job is for joinery work, as their oval profile is easier to hide than round-headed nails.

When nailing two pieces of wood together you should dovetail the nails as shown in the drawing, which will give the joint extra strength. When driving nails into wood, it will often split, especially when working near the end of a piece of timber. To prevent this happening, flatten the pointed end of the nail either with a file or by putting the head onto a brick or any hard surface and tapping the point flat. This stops the nail acting like a wedge, forcing the fibres of the wood apart or splitting it. The flattened end will cut through the wood knot and spread the wood fibres so that there is less chance of the wood splitting. Any nail can have the point flattened and will act in the same way. Round-headed nails are generally used for rougher work about the house and garden.

Screws

Sizes of screw are given by the length and size of the head. Common sizes are 6, 8 and 10 by whatever length you require. There are different types of head, with either a simple slot, Phillips or pozidrive designs—these have cross- or star-shaped finishes with four or eight turning points as opposed to the two of a slotted head. With a pozidrive there is less chance of the screwdriver slipping out and marking the wood.

For each size screw head you should use the correct size screwdriver, and one that is correctly ground. When screwing two pieces of wood together you must first drill a hole to clear the shank of the screw and, if using a countersunk screw, the wood must also be countersunk before inserting the screw so that the screw head finishes flush with the face of the wood. A pilot

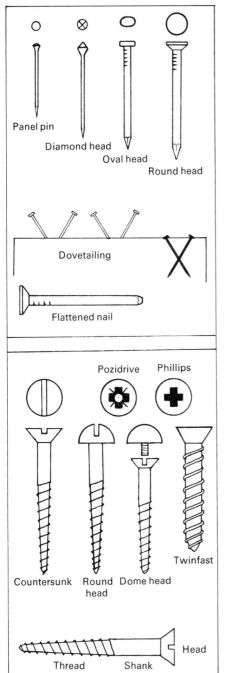

Panel pin

Diamond head

Oval head

Round head

Dovetailing

Flattened nail

Pozidrive   Phillips

Countersunk   Round head   Dome head

Twinfast

Thread   Shank   Head

hole should be made for easy entry.

When screwing into hardboard, rub the threaded part of the screw on a piece of soap or a candle. This will lubricate the screw so that it enters more easily and the head is less likely to be twisted off. This can often happen when using brass screws since they do not have the strength of their steel counterparts. However, they do not rust or discolour surrounding wood. One can also get zinc-plated screws, which withstand wet conditions inside or out and can look quite decorative.

A useful new addition to the screw family is the 'Twinfast' by GKN. This has two threads compared to one on the normal screw, and it has a parallel shank which makes it ideal for chipboard and other particle boards because it gives a very firm grip.

One other decorative screw in common use is the dome-headed screw, generally used for fixing mirrors. After the screw has been turned in, the threaded dome is screwed into the screw head giving a decorative finish and hiding the screw head at the same time. One point to remember when screwing a mirror to a wall is never to overtighten the screws, or the mirror may break.

So much for putting in screws, but what about removing a stubborn one? First remove any paint from the slot by scraping or tapping out with a bradawl. When this is completely clear put in a screwdriver of the correct size— one that fits the full width of the slot— and give the end of the screwdriver a tap with the hammer, while turning it at the same time. Once the screw has started to move, turn the screwdriver by hand to remove the screw.

Filling Holes

Holes in any type of surface look unsightly and hold dust and dirt so it is worth filling them as soon as possible. The method to be used varies according to the type of surface.

Wood

Wood tends to bruise easily and is often subject to man-made holes or defects in the natural timber. New wood, which has been bruised by a hammer dent, can usually be made good by putting a drop of water on the damaged area. This raises the grain and can be sandpapered smooth later. If the bruise or a shallow dent cannot be smoothed out by this method it will have to be filled with a fine grade filler. These are readily available in DIY shops and should be applied according to the manufacturer's instructions. Once the filler has dried the area should be rubbed smooth using fine sandpaper and a sanding block (Fig 1). Small holes, scratches and other defects are treated in the same manner.

This method is suitable only for surfaces which are going to be painted. If the wood is to be left natural you should add a dye to the filler to match the existing wood. The colour will lighten as the moisture dries out so experiment on an old piece of wood first to achieve the correct colour match. Alternatively, you could use

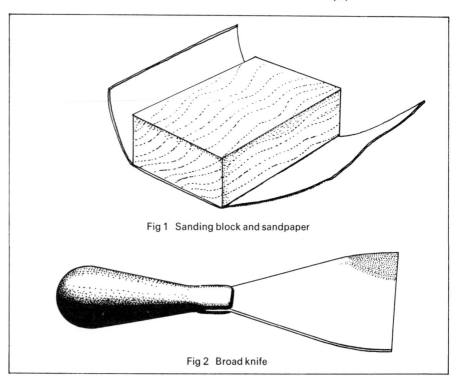

Fig 1 Sanding block and sandpaper

Fig 2 Broad knife

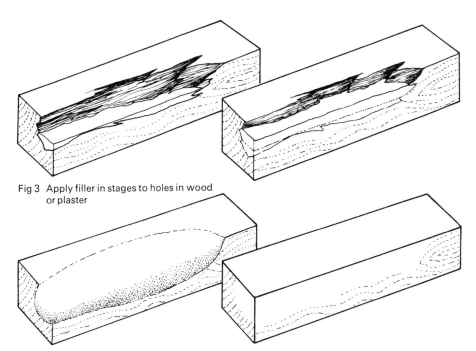

Fig 3 Apply filler in stages to holes in wood or plaster

Fig 4 Apply last layer of filler too thickly and smooth down to correct level

ready-made coloured fillers, but the disadvantage is that you are likely to finish up with three-quarters of the tin over, so it is worth experimenting with your own colours.

Many people use putty for filling holes in wood, but there is the problem that as the oil dries out the putty tends to shrink, leaving neat little depressions showing along the paintwork.

Plaster

Holes and defects, including cracks, in plaster can usually be filled with a cellulose filler. Cracks can be filled by using a broad knife (Fig 2), while larger holes will have to be built up in layers (Fig 3), waiting for each filling to dry before applying the next coat.

If you don't do this a depression will be left as the filler dries. You should also make the last coat a little too thick, leaving enough filler to smooth down to the level of the existing plaster (Fig 4).

When you are filling in holes on surfaces which are likely to be vibrated or shaken, such as doors, windows and frames, mix in a drop of PVA white woodworking adhesive with the filler as this will help the filler to hold better and be less liable to crack and fall out. When using a powder filler such as Polyfilla on any surface that is due to be painted, always apply two undercoats before putting on gloss paint. If you don't do this, you will get a matt finish to the gloss which shows the outline of the filled area.

Paint Preparation

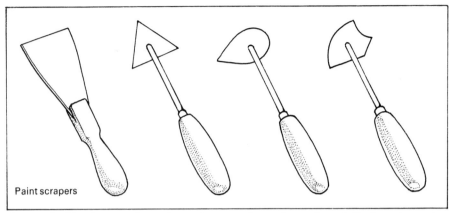

Paint scrapers

A great deal has been written about the techniques of painting, but it is often forgotten that even the most expert technique or expensive paint will be wasted if the object to be painted has not been properly prepared. So let us look at how to prepare some surfaces ready for painting.

New Wood

All the knots in the wood should be sealed with a proprietary brand of knotting sealer. This stops the resin in the knots from weeping out when the final coat of paint has been applied. You should then apply a good quality primer which is usually pink, white or yellow in colour. When this has dried rub down the surface with M2 grit sandpaper and fill any defects, such as nail holes, with putty or cellulose filler. The undercoats come next, and these should be of the correct colour for the final coats—this is usually specified on the tin containing the final colour. If the correct undercoat colour is not used this will affect the chosen colour, causing light or dark shading according to the undercoat used. Each undercoat, when dry, must be rubbed down before the next coat is applied. The final finish on the top coat is worth that little bit of extra labour.

Finally, apply the finishing coat, brushing well in the same direction to avoid drips and runs. If you are painting outside, wait for a fine, dry day, otherwise the gloss finishing-coat may bloom and dry dull.

Old Paintwork

Old paintwork will need particularly good rubbing down to remove any runs before you paint over it. It is best to use wet and dry emery paper, making sure that all flaking paint is removed and the edges are rubbed smooth. Do all the rubbing down first and dust off after completion. Two coats of undercoat will generally be required, especially if the finishing coat is a light colour.

It is sometimes necessary to remove old paintwork either by stripping or by burning. Burning is usually quicker, and ready-to-use gas lamps, which can be bought from a 'Do-It-Yourself' shop, are better than the old paraffin types. With gas you have a greater control over the heat output. Play the flame continuously backwards and forwards across the wood to prevent scorching. The idea is to remove the paint without burning the wood. *Do not* attempt to burn paint from facia and soffit boards, or near thatched roofs or asbestos, and take great care when working close to glass windows Chemical strippers are useful substitutes where heat cannot be applied, but be sure to follow exactly the manufacturer's instructions. After stripping with either heat or a commercial stripper, rub down the surface thoroughly and then proceed as for new wood.

Paint Application

Paint manufacturers have introduced new developments such as matt vinyl, sheen, gel, non-drip and a host of other names. Do not be confused by these words. There are two basic differences in finishing paints : they are either standard liquid paints or gel paints.

The gel or 'thixotropical' paints are perhaps the easiest to apply as they are less liable to drip or run off the brush and consequently avoid tears and sags once applied to a flat surface. When using liquid paints you must apply them evenly onto the surface, otherwise the paint will run leaving ugly tear marks. Since this does not happen when using gel paints they are much more easily applied than the liquid type.

Should you need to strain paint you will find it easiest to place a stocking over the can to be strained and to pour through the stocking into a clean empty can. This method is much cleaner and easier than the traditional one of tying a stocking over the clean can and then pouring the paint.

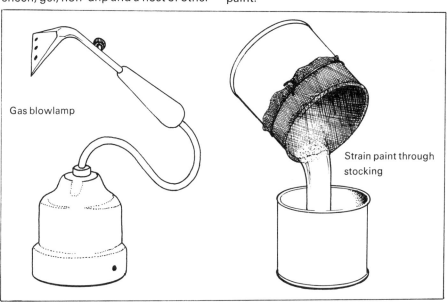

Gas blowlamp

Strain paint through stocking

Wallpaper

Much has been written about the art of wallpapering, but recent developments by manufacturers have meant a number of changes in technique. In addition to the old-style papers, which had to be pasted before hanging, there are now ready-pasted wallpapers which you just dip into a trough of water, and vinyl papers where one pastes the walls rather than the back of the paper. Despite these changes which have made things a lot easier, you will not get a pleasing end result if you do not set about the job in the right manner.

Choosing the best place to start is sometimes the most difficult decision. This will vary from room to room, so here are a few rule of thumb guides. Try to start from the lightest part of the room, near a window for instance. If you are going to use a large-patterned wallpaper start over a chimney-breast or a main focal point of the room, and set out the paper from the centre of the chosen spot in order to achieve an equal pattern on either side (Fig 1). When cutting the wallpaper to length you may find that you will waste less paper if you use two rolls side by side ; this is especially so when using large-patterned wallpapers. Always try to finish the wallpaper in the darkest part of the room.

Another important point is to make sure the wallpaper is upright. The easiest way of doing this is to mark an upright line with either a level or a plumb-bob (Fig 2). A plumb-bob can easily be made by tying a nut or any weight to the end of a piece of string ; when this is suspended it will automatically give an upright line. Do not try to wrap wallpaper around internal or external angles. Cut the paper 10mm ($\frac{3}{8}$in) oversize and just overlap the remaining piece (Figs 3, 4). If you are hanging vinyl wallpaper use either Copydex or Solvite overlap paste as ordinary wallpaper paste will not adhere to vinyl.

Sizing

It must be stressed that the walls should be fully prepared before you attempt to apply wallpaper. Holes, cracks and any other defects to the plaster must be made good. The wall will then need to be sized (sealed) so that the wallpaper when pasted will slide into position. If the walls are not

Fig 2 Home-made plumb-bob

sized and you attempt to put the wallpaper straight on, because the plaster is porous it will suck the paste from the wallpaper, making it impossible to move the paper into position.

Sizing the room can be done by diluting wallpaper paste or by buying a proprietary size and mixing it according to the manufacturer's instructions. When this is applied to the walls it will form a seal so that as you begin to hang the wallpaper it will slide easily into position.

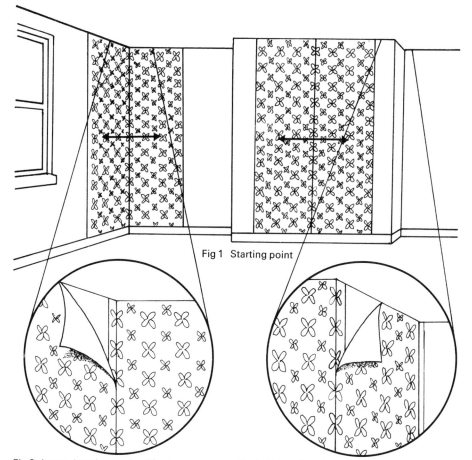

Fig 1 Starting point

Fig 3 Internal angle : overlap 10mm

Fig 4 External angle : overlap 10mm

Removing Wallpaper

When removing wallpaper you will need to use water to make the job easier. Therefore take care when working close to any open electricity sockets—it is advisable to turn off the electricity before you begin.

Wallpaper should first be soaked with water. When this has penetrated through the paper it can be removed easily with a broad knife.

Washable wallpapers need to be scratched before water is applied ; use a coarse grade of sandpaper to break the surface of the paper. Washable wallpapers are the most difficult of all papers to remove, so extra time should be allowed for the water to soak through and penetrate.

If washable wallpapers are the most difficult to remove, Vinyl wallpapers are the easiest. Starting at one corner, lift the film of vinyl and pull off each piece which will leave the backing paper still stuck to the wall. This may be left on to act as a lining paper, or removed with water in the conventional way.

13

Fixing into Masonry

Drilling

Drilling into brick and plaster often seems a difficult task, but there are a number of tips which can make it much easier. The first essential is to have either a hand or electric drill ; the other important tool is the drill bit itself, which must be specifically designed for masonry. This has a very hard tip on the end, making it easier to drill into bricks, plaster, concrete and stone. It is important to ensure that the drill size is correct for the size of screw being used. A number 10 is the most common one in use.

After fixing the drill bit into the chuck of the drill, put the tip onto the point where the hole is going to be and turn it slowly so that it goes through the plaster into the brick. After a start has been made, you can increase the speed, but pull the drill out at intervals to clear any brick dust. Always drill 5mm ($\frac{1}{4}$in) deeper than the length of the screw, this allows a small clearance for debris when inserting the plug. If you are using an electric drill the same procedure applies ; use the slow speed if you have a two-speed drill, and once the hole is started use a pump action —pushing the drill in and withdrawing it at intervals—to remove the brick dust from the hole. Some electric drills have a hammer action which allows the drill bit to cut more rapidly, but care must be taken when starting the hole as the drill bit tends to jump and skid until entry is made.

It is possible to drill into brick without using a drill bit. Take two 60mm ($2\frac{1}{2}$in) oval nails and cut the heads off with a hack-saw. Put them into the drill chuck, and drill into the brick. The nails will twist together forming a spiral, and a number of holes can be made with them before they need to be replaced. Nails are especially useful when drilling into building blocks since these are softer than bricks. You may find that some old plasters containing lime are much softer than modern types. If this is the case stick a piece of sellotape over the point where the hole is to be drilled to stop the plaster crumbling away as you drill.

Inserting a Plug

Before putting a screw into masonry you must insert a plug for the screw to bite into. Individual plastic plugs are the best and most readily available. They come in different sizes for different screws, and the most useful ones are the universal types that will fit three or four different screw sizes. After selecting the size required, push it into the hole and tap it home so that the plug is approximately 3mm ($\frac{1}{8}$in) below the surface of the plaster. This is to ensure that when the screw is driven in, expanding the plug, the plaster around the edge of the hole does not crumble away.

One point to remember is that when fixing cupboards or shelves to the wall always use screws long enough to carry their weight when they are full ! Screws fixed only into the plaster will not hold securely enough.

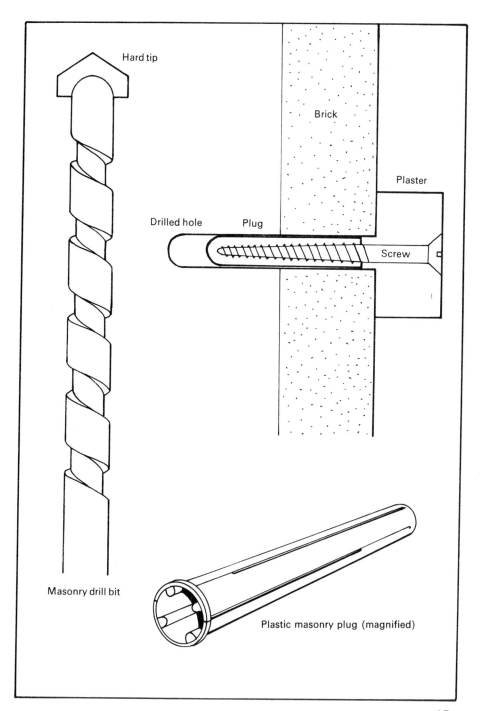

Hard tip

Brick

Plaster

Drilled hole   Plug

Screw

Masonry drill bit

Plastic masonry plug (magnified)

15

Fixing a Shelf

It is often necessary to put up shelves, particularly when you have just moved into a new house or flat—there just never seems to be enough shelf space. How often have your shelves sagged or fallen down, either because the wrong material was used or because the screws were too short ? As with every sort of home maintenance or repair, it is never worth doing a cheap or quick job.

There are now many shelving systems available in which you screw a pair of slotted uprights to the wall and clip on the shelf brackets. This type of shelving is very easy to use but do remember to put enough screws into the upright to secure the shelves well into the wall. One tends to forget just how much books weigh, and if the uprights are not securely fixed the whole lot will tumble down.

Fitting shelves into a recess is not difficult since you do not have to put up any side pieces to take the supports for the shelves to rest on (Fig 1). If the shelf is to take heavy loads such as books then you should fit a bearer along the back as well as the ends. The bearer can be of timber sized about 75 × 50mm (3 × 2in) or you may wish to use aluminium angle (Fig 2). The

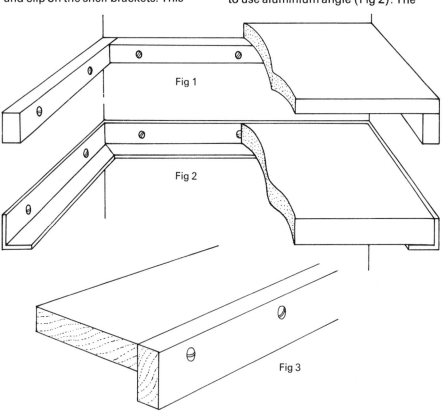

Fig 1

Fig 2

Fig 3

latter makes a neat unobtrusive job. The shelf should be of solid timber, such as Parana pine. Avoid particle boards since they tend to sag. On longer lengths the shelves can be strengthened by screwing a strip of solid timber along the front edge (Fig 3). This has the additional advantage of giving a neater looking shelf as it will cover the ends of the bearers.

To fit a shelf into a recess it must obviously be cut to fit precisely. One good way to do this is as follows : first of all measure and cut the shelf 25mm (1 in) longer than required and then place it into the recess. With a compass opened to 12mm ($\frac{1}{2}$in) scratch a line on the shelf following the precise shape of the wall (Fig 4). Use a panel saw to cut along this line. Before you measure the other end, cut a thin lath to the exact size of the recess ; this will prevent you from cutting the shelf too short or leaving it long if your measurements are inaccurate. Then, with one end of the lath flush with the cut end of the shelf, make a pencil mark at the uncut end at the opposite end of the lath (Fig 5). Put the shelf back into the recess, set the compass to the pencil line and scratch the shape of the wall onto the shelf. When this is cut the shelf will fit like a glove.

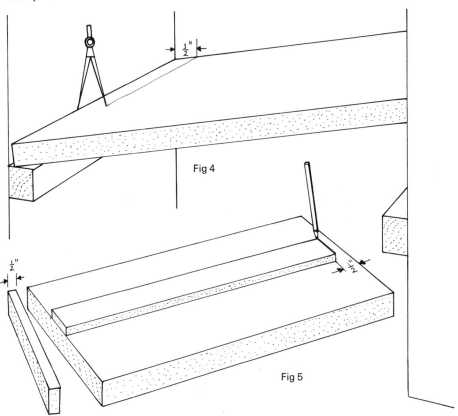

Fig 4

Fig 5

Floorboards

Creaking Floorboards

How many times have you tried to creep home at the dead of night only to be detected on the last step by the infernal creaking stair or floorboard? Well, never again, because there are cures for horrific creaks!

There are several causes for these: staircases and floorboards are usually made of timber, and there will always be a shrinkage factor due to the timber drying out, thus opening joints in floorboards and sometimes breaking glued joints, as in a staircase. Even when the timber has finished drying out there will always be a certain amount of movement due to the humidity in the air. Have you noticed how a door which sticks in winter will shut quite freely in the summer? This type of movement occurs year in year out.

Another reason for movement, creaks and groans is that heating pipes may be fixed too close to the underside of the floorboards. This has two effects: firstly, the continual heating and cooling of a domestic heating system adds to the movement of the wood; secondly, if the pipes actually touch the underside of the floorboard, it will expand as the pipes heat and contract as they cool, thus causing creaks. The cure for this is to lift the floorboard and cut away the wood where the pipe actually touches it,

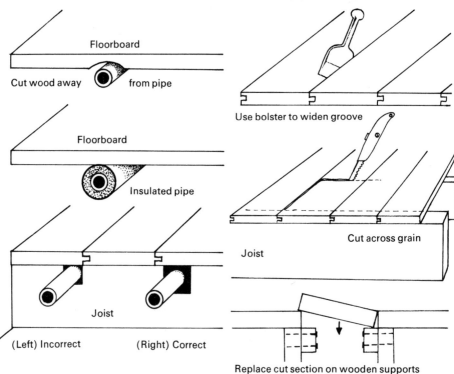

Floorboard

Cut wood away — from pipe

Floorboard

Insulated pipe

Joist

(Left) Incorrect   (Right) Correct

Use bolster to widen groove

Cut across grain

Joist

Replace cut section on wooden supports

taking care not to cut through to the face of the board. You should also inspect the notched cut-out in the joist to make sure that the pipe is not touching the sides of the notch. If so, fit a piece of heat-resistant rubber to form an expansion area. You may have to cut the notch wider to do this, but do not cut away more than is absolutely necessary as this will weaken the joist. When the offending pipes have been checked and put right, nail down the boards. Once again you should take care, as a nail in the wrong position may result in a burst pipe.

Floorboards are usually nailed down with the nails punched just below the surface. To eliminate creaks, go over each board and check that all the nails are hammered home and punched in. If not, go over the whole floor punching in these nails. (This will result in dust rising from the joints so cover any furniture you have in the room with dust sheets.) If you add any nails to the floorboard beware of what could be underneath, eg wires and pipes. It is worth remembering that screws will have greater holding power than nails.

A very good tip to stop noisy floorboards is to sprinkle talcum powder liberally into the joints of the floor. This acts as a lubricant and it is an amazingly easy way of eliminating noisy floorboards.

Removing a Floorboard

Removing a floorboard is a job that often needs to be done when renovating a house, when you want to add an extra power point, or put in a water pipe. Very often you can see split boards where someone has shoved a tyre lever or something similar into the joint without thinking, and then just heaved it.

There is a better method, which is not only easier but cheaper, since you won't have the expense of buying a new piece of timber to replace the board taken out. You will need a metal bolster and a Stanley knife with a wood sawblade fixed in the handle. Most floorboards are tongue and groove so place the bolster in the groove and hit it with a hammer until you break through the tongue. This gap will enable you to insert the sawblade. Take care as there may be wires or pipes under the board and it is advisable to switch off the electricity at the meter. If you do come across a pipe when sawing, stop immediately.

Cut along the tongue until you reach the joist, then gently and gradually turn the saw, cutting at the same time so that you cut across the grain along the side of the joist. Cut 20mm ($\frac{3}{4}$in) into the next board, so as to sever the tongue to allow the board to be lifted out easily.

Repeat the cut across the end grain at the side of the next joist. Three sides of the board are now cut, so sliding the bolster into the cut tongue, gently pop out the board. Of course, when you replace the board it will drop through as there are no supports; to prevent this nail two pieces of 50 × 25mm (2 × 1in) wood which are 50mm (2in) wider than the width of the floorboard to the joist. The cut board will now be supported and can be nailed back after the wire or pipes have been run.

The Staircase

A staircase is a major contributor to creaks and squeaks. It is usually made up of three main parts : the strings, which are the two side pieces, and the treads and risers, which are supported by them (see diagram). In time, as the timber shrinks, there may be movement, and when pressure is put on the tread a creaking noise can often be heard. To stop this you must be able to get at the underside of the staircase, which is not always the easiest of jobs since the cupboard which is usually found under the stairs often houses electricity meters, gas meters and all sorts of household junk.

Once the area is cleared you will probably have to remove either a piece of hardboard or plasterboard that will be nailed to the two edges of the strings. Take care as this will need to be replaced when the job is finished. Gently prise the board away, starting from one edge and working down, releasing the nails as you go. When this has been removed and the underside of the staircase exposed, use a vacuum cleaner to remove all dust and debris. This will make for cleaner working conditions, and stop you having to work with dust and dirt falling around you.

You will now see that the treads and risers are held in position by wedges ; check to see if any are loose or missing. If so, remove the loose ones, one at a time, and apply PVA woodworking adhesive to both sides of the wedge. Then replace them and knock them home with a hammer, using a piece of scrap wood to avoid bruising the

timber. Knock the tread into the string and do the same with the riser.

Working on one tread and riser at a time, the next operation is to check the angle blocks, which should be fixed between the top of the tread and the riser. If they are loose, remove them, put on some woodworking adhesive, and hold them in position with a small nail until the adhesive dries. Make sure that the nail does not stick through either the tread or the riser. If there are no blocks on the staircase, cut some out from scrap wood and fix them as already described. The last job to do before nailing back the piece which has been removed is to punch in the nails that hold the bottom of the riser to the back of the tread.

Modernizing the Staircase

Modernizing an old staircase is a job well within the scope of most people. The most popular way of doing this is to board in the banisters, and this is best done using plywood rather than hardboard, which tends to buckle easily. This form of modernization incorporates the stair rails, but you may wish to have a more open aspect by removing the rails and fitting in a new wide rail to the top part of the handrail.

The only point to watch here is to make sure you do not cover up or destroy a nice piece of existing wood. If your staircase is of a particularly nice wood you can, of course, strip off any old paint, thus allowing the natural beauty of the wood to show. Many staircases look very attractive when treated in this manner.

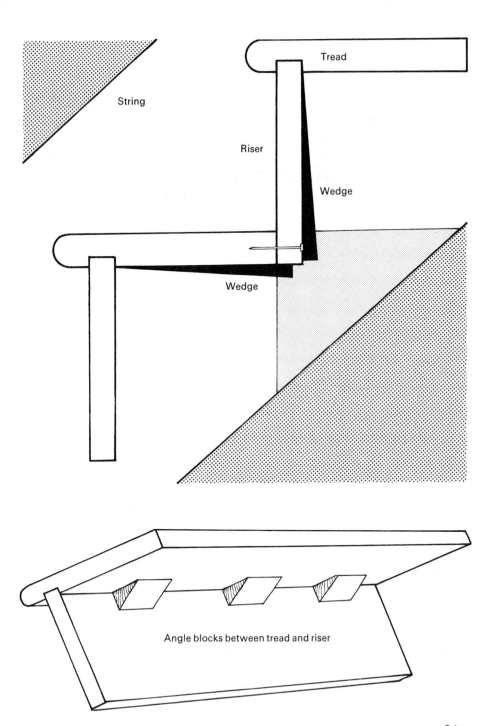

String

Tread

Riser

Wedge

Wedge

Angle blocks between tread and riser

21

Fixing a Plug

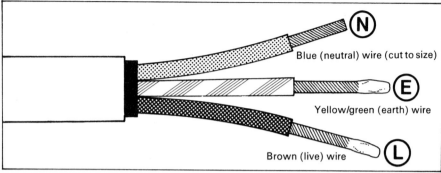

Blue (neutral) wire (cut to size)

Yellow/green (earth) wire

Brown (live) wire

All appliances such as washing machines, vacuum cleaners and food mixers need to be connected to a plug. All new installations are now square-pin 13 amp, although if your house is fairly old you may still have round-pin 15 amp fixtures. However, any appliance needs to be wired to a plug whether it is a square-pin or a round-pin and this must be done in the correct manner.

There are many different makes of plug on the market and they vary considerably in price. Choose a good quality plug (a name brand) and make sure that it is suitable for your purpose; for example an electric fire or fan heater must have a plug that will take the amount of wattage stated on the appliance. Do check this carefully with your local supplier.

After purchasing the plug look at the wires on the appliance; you will normally find three : yellow and green stripe (*earth*) brown (*live*) and blue (*neutral*). Quite often these wires will have soldered ends and in most cases they are longer than required. First they must be trimmed to the correct length, and it does not matter if you

cut off the soldered ends. Cut the wires so that the outer casing covering the three coloured wires is inside the plug and held in the clamp provided. Then secure each wire in turn as in the diagram, making sure that it is held tight. Loose wires can lead to arcing which will cause heat and eventually fire.

The most important wire is the earth —green and yellow stripes—which must be connected to the correct terminal. The live wire (brown) is connected to the fuse side of the plug ; you may find that you have to remove the fuse to do this. The neutral (blue) is connected to the remaining terminal.

Check the screws for tightness and clamp the outer casing to the inside of the plug. After checking that all screws are right, make sure that you have fitted the correct fuse—13 amp for washing machines, vacuum cleaners, or fan heaters, 3 amp for lighting. Check the fuse rating for each individual piece of electrical equipment when you buy it. It is wise to keep some spare fuses handy for any failure or emergency. The final thing is to replace the top of the plug.

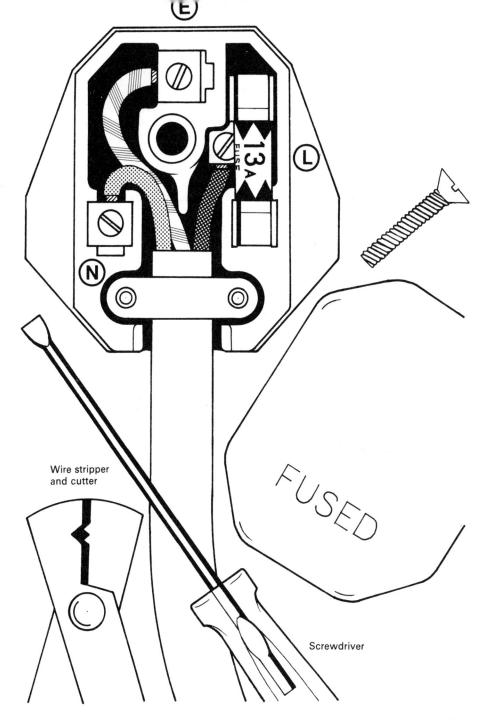

Wire stripper
and cutter

Screwdriver

FUSED

E

L

N

13A
FUSE

Mending a Fuse

Suddenly the whole house is plunged into darkness. The television goes off, the lights go out. Your first thought probably is that there has been a power cut ; but all the other houses have their lights on, so a blown fuse must be the answer. There may then follow some minutes' confusion as you struggle to find a torch, or a candle, and the necessary items needed to repair the fuse that has blown.

Well, that little scene has probably happened to everyone at some time, so be warned and be prepared. Electrical fuses are like a safety valve : if a circuit is overloaded then the fuse will break and not the appliance. It is wise to make sure you know what to do while it is still light, so that you are prepared for any failure in a domestic fuse system. First you need to know where the fuse board is : under the stairs is a popular place, or in the garage.

Once the fuse board is located, check what type of fuse you have ; you may find that you have the cartridge-type fuse (Fig 1) or contact breaker (Fig 2), neither of which requires fuse wire. With cartridge fuses you only need to keep spare fuses of the correct rating, which is usually stamped on the plastic holder. Keep two of each type as spares. The contact breaker needs no fuses : if it has blown just press the button to make contact again.

The most common fuse is the type which uses wire (Fig 3). It is a good idea to keep an insulated screwdriver, torch, candle and fuse wire of the correct rating beside the fuse box. If a

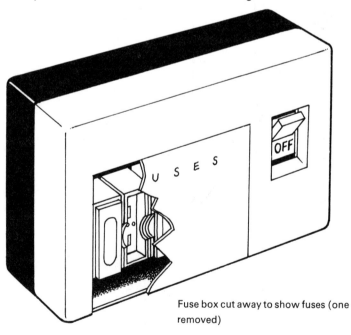

Fuse box cut away to show fuses (one removed)

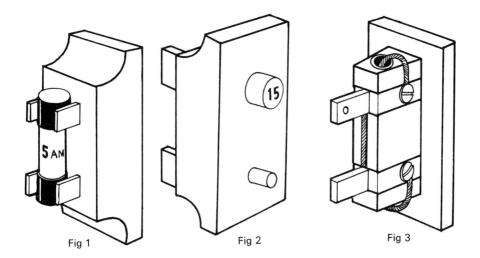

Fig 1   Fig 2   Fig 3

wire-type fuse blows, first turn off the electricity at the fuse box—there is usually a large switch marked 'on' and 'off'. Remove the fuse cover and then the blown fuse by gripping the top and bottom and easing it until it comes free. Release the old fuse wire by undoing the two screws. Thread new wire, wrapping it around the screw heads, and tighten them up (a little vaseline on the contacts will help ease entry). Replace the fuse and fuse cover, and switch on. Make sure you replace the screwdriver and other tools.

Important—never use a fuse wire of a higher rating, and always turn off the electricity before removing a fuse. If the fuse continues to blow, call in a qualified electrician.

Repairing an Electric Kettle

Another very simple household repair you can easily do yourself is renewing the element of an electric kettle. If the kettle has just stopped working, first of all check that the over-ride switch

has not tripped ; this switch is found at the socket end of the kettle. Push the plug firmly into the kettle ; if the plug does not engage properly, reconnect the trip switch by pushing it in firmly. If the plug pushes in easily then the element in the kettle is probably at fault, but before taking the kettle to pieces check that the fuse at the mains plug has not blown.

Once you are sure that the fuse is not at fault, unplug the kettle from the main supply. Hold the kettle firmly and with your free hand unscrew the plug socket, and when this has been unscrewed make a note of how it is assembled : remembering this will help you to put back the new element in exactly the same way. You will notice that there are two washers, one inside and one outside, which make the waterproof joint. After removing the old element, replace the new one in exactly the same manner. Before plugging into the mains, check for any leaks.

25

Windows (1)

Windows which will not shut or which will not open are everyday problems. One of the major difficulties with wooden windows is that they are affected by the weather and the amount of humidity in the air. Another common reason for windows which stick is too much paint which has been applied over the years. Successive coats build up and then eventually jam. So let us look at prevention of and cures for some of the most common faults in the different kinds of window.

Wooden Windows

With wooden windows, it makes no difference whether they are double-glazed or not, the treatment is similar. Normally wood windows come ready primed (see Paint Preparation). They will need two undercoats and one gloss coat. When painting do make sure that the paint does not build up on the edges. Always brush the edges of windows well with the paint brush.

Old wooden windows with excessive paint on them will need the paint

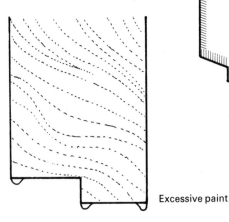

Avoid build-up of paint on edges

Excessive paint

26

removed down to the bare wood (see Old Paintwork). Once the paint has been removed check that the window operates satisfactorily—some of the wood may have to be shaved off to make it fit properly. Use a surform for this, remembering that in winter the window will have expanded slightly due to humidity, so do not shave off too much wood. Check that the hinges and catches are operating properly— if not, remove and soak them in penetrating oil, cleaning them thoroughly before fixing back to the frame and window.

Metal Windows

Metal windows bring their own type of problems. Paint can be removed from them only by using a paint stripper. If movement has taken place due to settlement of a house the only way to shave them down is with a metal file. One is available to fit the surform but since metal windows are dipped and galvanized this operation will, of course, remove this protective coat, and you should apply a proprietary rust inhibitor to all exposed metal parts. Read the manufacturer's instructions before buying and make absolutely sure that the rust preventer can be painted over. Maintenance of metal windows includes removing any rust spots with a file and wire brush, after which rust preventer should be applied. When this has been completed treat all metal work with metal primer paint, and then continue the normal painting procedure as with wood windows. Aluminium and plastic are being used increasingly for windows. These need little maintenance, except an occasional wash down with warm soapy water, and never need painting.

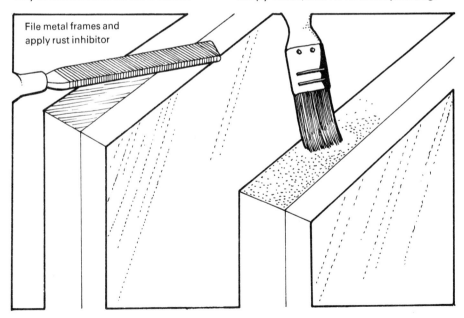

File metal frames and apply rust inhibitor

Windows (2)

Sash Cords

Sash windows suffer from the same problems as casement windows, as they are also made of wood and are still fitted in thousands of houses. The one additional maintenance job with this type of window is to check the cords by which the windows are counterbalanced. Over the years these will need replacing. The easiest way to do this is to start by gently prising the stop bead away from the frame using a flat chisel. Lever from the back of the stop bead so that you avoid bruising the paint and wood on the face edge, and remove the stop bead on the opposite side in the same way.

If the two sash cords are broken remove the sash from the frame or, if you cannot do this easily, cut the cord and gently lower the sash weight into the cavity. Even if you only need to replace one cord it may be worth replacing all four; the reason will become obvious when—after you have carefully replaced one cord—another one breaks a few weeks later and you have to repeat the work all over again.

Remove the broken cord ends from the sash (Fig 1). Then remove the parting bead (Fig 2), using the same procedure as for the stop bead. This will expose the pocket through which the weights can be removed, and this is also prised out. Then remove the sash weights and the broken piece of cord. The two pieces of cord can be put together to give you the length of new cord; otherwise you should measure from the bottom of the sash to the bottom of the cord groove and

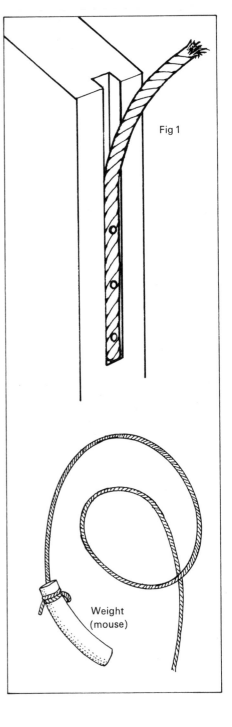

Fig 1

Weight (mouse)

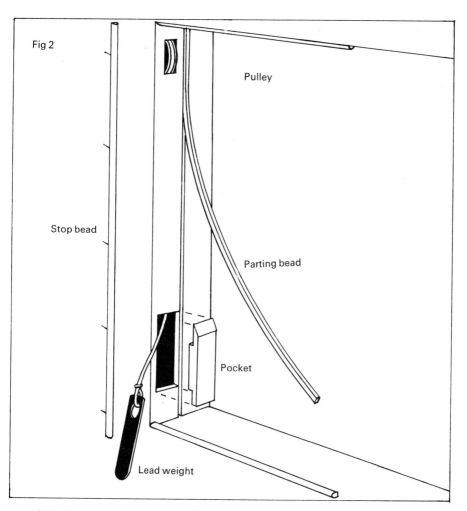

Fig 2

Pulley

Stop bead

Parting bead

Pocket

Lead weight

mark that measurement onto the frame with a pencil, taking care to ensure that the cord is not too long—so that the sash will not open fully—or too short—so that you cannot close the sash.

Then, using a 'mouse' (a weighted piece of string) thread this over the pulley, lower it into the pocket and tie it to some good quality sash cord. Pull this up over the pulley, remove the string, and tie on the sash weight. Then pull the weight up and down by hand to ensure free movement of the pulley, making sure you pull it right up to the top of the sash. When you have cut the cord to the right length replace the pocket and parting bead.

Fix the cord to the frame with a 25mm (1in) round-headed nail then cut the cord at the pencil mark which you made earlier. Fix the cord into the groove on the sash using nails or staples, and replace the stop bead to complete the job.

Replacing a Glass Pane

Almost every home suffers a broken pane of glass at some time ; replacing the glass in a wood or metal window creates no great problem and you should follow the same procedure in both cases. However, if you have aluminium or double-glazed windows, these are best left to experts to repair.

Either measure the broken pane from rebate to rebate (Fig 1), and take off about 3–4mm ($\frac{1}{8}$in) so that the pane will fit in neatly, or cut a piece of newspaper or cardboard to make a pattern. Take the measurements or the pattern to a glass merchant who will cut the glass to the correct size. It is important to give him the exact thickness of the glass you require, particularly if you are replacing glass in a rise and fall sash window. Take a piece of the broken glass with you so that the glass merchant knows what thickness and weight to give you, as this type of window relies on counterbalanced weights, and different weights of glass will affect the operation of the window.

With the glass cut to size, break out the remaining pieces of old glass, taking extreme care. Clean out all the old putty with a chisel, leaving no high spots, and remove any small nails. Once this has been done, prime the rebate with wood primer or, if you are working on a metal window, use metal primer. Metal windows have spring clips instead of nails, which should be removed and put somewhere safe as you will need them for replacing the glass.

Before you put in any putty, check the glass for size by placing the pane into the rebates. If it is correct, place a bed of putty all around the rebates. The putty should be soft and easy to work ; if it is too sticky add a small amount of powdered Polyfilla. This will stiffen it and stop it sticking to your fingers. Do not use old putty with lumps in or you may break the glass when bedding it in. Put the glass into the rebate and press gently against the putty with a rag. Any putty that squeezes out round the edges can be trimmed off later. Using 15mm ($\frac{1}{2}$in) panel pins fix one on each side of the glass, and tap them home with a small hammer, sliding this down the glass (Fig 2). This will secure the glass until the putty sets. On metal windows use putty made especially for metal windows (not linseed oil putty) and secure the glass with the spring clips removed earlier.

Now, using your thumb, press a thin roll of putty on top of the glass along the rebate all around the window, and then smooth this to a neat angle using a putty knife. It makes it easier to get a smooth finish if you dip the putty knife into some water, and you can erase any bumps with a soft dry paint brush. All that you have to do now is leave the putty to set for approximately fourteen days, and then paint it the required colours.

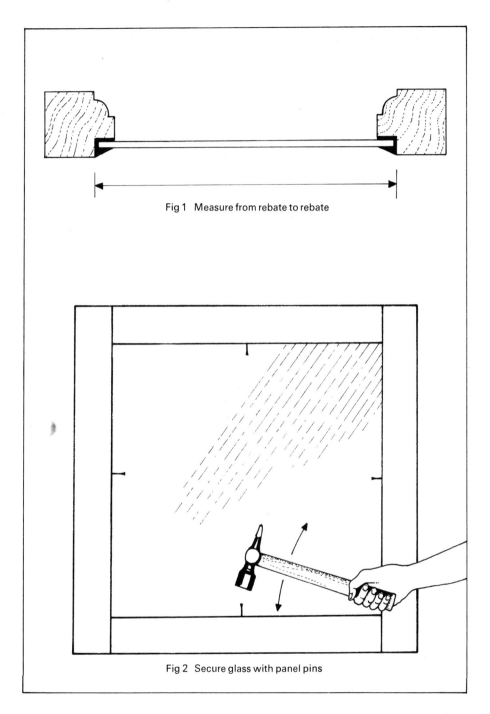

Fig 1 Measure from rebate to rebate

Fig 2 Secure glass with panel pins

Cutting Glass

Instruments

Most people when asked if they can cut a piece of glass shudder at the very thought of a hardened steel wheel scoring across glass, but I shall try to dispel any worries you may have about glass cutting.

First you need a glass cutter. There are several types available; the most common in general use is a hardened steel wheel that leaves a scratch line as it revolves over the glass. A more expensive version of this is a tungsten wheel which has a very much longer life due to the extra hardness of the wheel. This type of wheel, however, does not leave such a clean scratch line as the hardened steel wheel.

There are, of course, diamond cutters, which have a small industrial diamond inserted into a handle (to give leverage) and to enable the user to score the glass. Contrary to most people's belief the diamond cutter is the most difficult cutter to use and only practice will enable the user to cut glass successfully.

For the purpose of this book we will use the hardened steel wheel cutter. The wheel of the cutter must always be able to revolve, so a light oil is used to lubricate it. A piece of sponge in a jar, impregnated with a light oil, will serve as a dip for the glass cutter (Fig 1), and should be used after every scribe. It is

Fig 1 Using a glass cutter

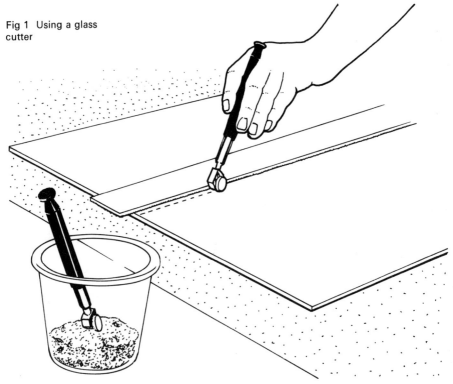

kitchen table, and with a straight edge score the wood with a Stanley knife along the marked line. Do this round the door on both sides. (Sometimes the piece to be cut off is not completely straight so remember to allow for this on the other side.) This will stop the paint chipping or the veneer splitting when you cut. Using a panel-saw cut along the scored line, keeping just on the waste side (Fig 3). Then smooth the edges with sandpaper and rehang the door using the wedge for support.

Warped Doors

Badly fitted doors or doors which have warped will cause all sorts of problems.

Warping will cause doors to jam ; the locks will not fit into their keeps and this also makes entry for any intruder that much easier.

It is not a simple job to refit doors that are twisted and warped ; therefore prevention is the best cure. There are various ways to avoid warping : always paint or lacquer the door as soon as it is hung—not forgetting the top of the door—and be sure to paint the bottom edge before hanging the door. This is particularly important on any outside door. Doors which are waiting to be hung should be stored flat to avoid any warping before hanging, and if you are fixing laminate to a door always laminate both sides ; if this is not done warping will almost certainly occur.

But what if you have a door which is already warped—how can you put it back into shape ? Unfortunately the success rate is low, though you can try these methods : wedge the door as shown (Fig 4), leaving it for as long as possible—for instance while you are away on holiday. Another method is to try 'throwing the hinges', by letting in one hinge more deeply and pushing out the other (Fig 5), so that the door can shut even though it is still twisted.

An unpainted wood door which has warped can be liberally sprinkled with water on both sides and then laid across battens and weighted with bricks to try and counteract the warping (Fig 6), then left for a few days to dry. This should remove the twist. The wood will need to be rubbed down with sandpaper as the water will raise the grain, and it should be painted as soon as possible.

Lubrication of Wood

Anything made of wood, such as drawers, doors and windows, is liable to expand or contract because of changes in humidity, and if you plane off any of the wood to ease it, you may find that when it shrinks again draughty windows or loose drawers may occur. However, it is easy and very quick to overcome these problems. Runners and the sides of a drawer can be rubbed with either soap or a candle ; never use linseed oil, which tends to go sticky and makes the drawer jam worse than before, or engine oil, as this will stain the wood and collect dust.

Washing-up liquid has many uses other than simply washing dishes. A spot of liquid on a hinge will instantly stop any squeak and the hinge may be wiped afterwards so that you don't have the mark or greasy stain which often occurs with conventional oils. But don't use this liquid on locks.

Burst Pipes

Should you be so unlucky as to have a burst pipe there are several things you must do very quickly, if you are at home at the time, although invariably pipes seem to burst when you are out of the house or away on holiday.

Proper insulation will safeguard against this disaster, but should a burst occur the first job is to turn off the water supply. Usually, the cold stop tap will be found under the sink, and the hot in the airing cupboard, but it is worth making sure that you know where they are in your own home. Also check that the taps can be turned, for they can get very stiff, and a regular check is obviously essential—just imagine water pouring through the ceiling with you unable to turn the tap off!

If there is a leak or burst pipe in the hot water system, you should immediately turn off the immersion heater or shut off the boiler, to prevent any further expansion of hot water. Turn off the main stop cock to the hot water, usually found in the airing cupboard, and open all the hot water taps in the house to let the surplus water drain away. Once the water has been cleared from the affected area, work can begin.

Replacing a small section of pipe is quite difficult so I suggest that you use a proprietary flexible copper connector, which makes the job of connecting two pieces of pipe relatively easy. There is nothing worse than having a catastrophe and not being able to do anything about it because you lack the necessary equipment, so it is advisable to buy one of these and keep it for such an emergency, just as you would an electrical fuse. These connectors come complete with instructions, and after you have cut out the split section of pipe, they take no more than five minutes to connect.

After the new piece of pipe has been installed, turn all the taps off before turning on the water supply. When the main valve has been turned on, release any air trapped in the pipes by undoing all the taps until the water runs evenly. Check for leaks and if all is well turn the immersion heater on again, and reset the boiler.

If the leak is on the cold water system, turn off the main stop cock, which is usually under the kitchen sink. Turn on all cold taps to release any trapped water and when the water ceases to run proceed with the repair in exactly the same way as already described.

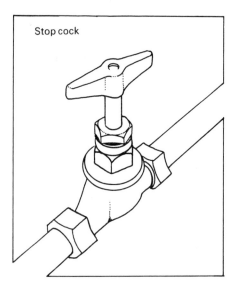

Stop cock

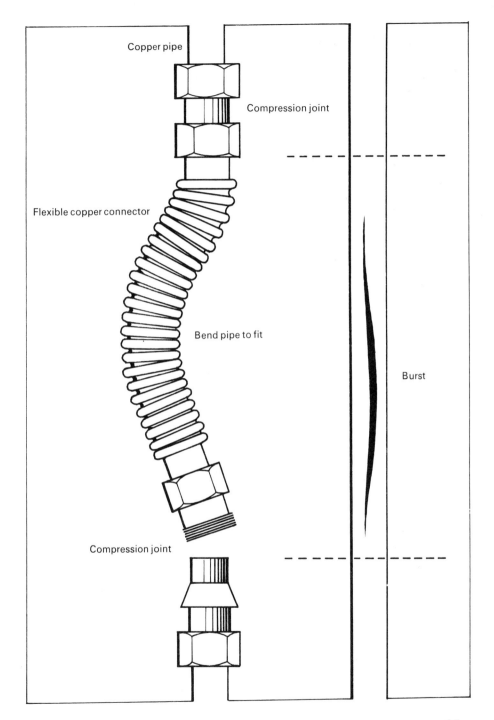

Copper pipe

Compression joint

Flexible copper connector

Bend pipe to fit

Burst

Compression joint

Unblocking a Pipe

We must all have suffered at one time from a blocked pipe either in the sink, waste pipe or any of the other pipes which run in the average house. Let us look at ways we can avoid blockages in the first place ; then at how to remove an obstruction should one occur. The most frequent problem area is the kitchen sink—just think how much debris goes down the waste pipe. Remember that prevention is always better than cure, so do not force potato peelings, carrots, or tea leaves down the sink—put them on the compost heap.

If a blockage does occur you will need the following : a rubber plunger, a length of fencing wire—about 3mm ($\frac{1}{8}$in) in diameter—and a pair of pipe grips. The rubber plunger is ideal for dealing with slight blockages. Fill the sink with 25mm (1in) of water and

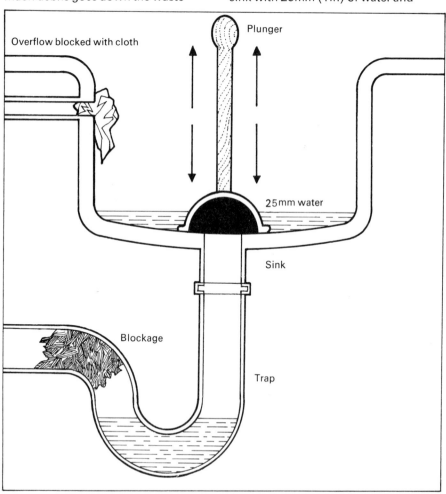

Overflow blocked with cloth

Plunger

25mm water

Sink

Blockage

Trap

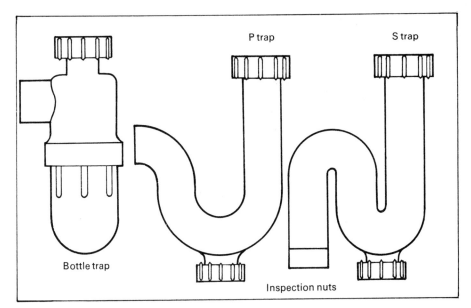

P trap

S trap

Bottle trap

Inspection nuts

block the overflow with a dish cloth. This will need to be held firmly in place because air and water will try to escape via the overflow as you apply pressure with the plunger. If the overflow is uncovered a smelly and soggy result will occur. With the dish cloth held in place, position the rubber plunger over the waste outlet and press sharply down, forcing air at pressure into the outlet. Several pumps with the plunger will normally clear minor obstructions.

If this fails you will have to look under the sink for the trap, which acts as an airlock to stop unpleasant smells coming up the pipe from the drain. There are many different types of traps and the most common are shown in the diagrams. All will have an inspection nut that can be removed with a pair of pliers. Place a bucket underneath and then remove the nut to see if the blockage is in the trap. If it is, remove

it through the inspection nut. Failing this take off the whole trap assembly and dismantle all the components. Remove any debris and clean all the parts thoroughly before reassembling.

If the blockage is in the actual pipe leading to the drain the trap must be removed and fencing wire put down the pipe. Bend the first 10mm ($\frac{1}{2}$in) of wire so that it can be used as a hook. This method will usually remove any obstruction lodged in the pipe. Once the pipe is clear and the trap screwed back in place flush the pipe through with clean water.

It is worthwhile remembering that the overflow of any sink or basin will block up over a period of time, and then if you leave a tap running there will be a minor disaster. From time to time use a thin gauge wire to clear any soap residue, hair or other obstruction and flush through, using an old plastic bottle full of clean water.

39

Tap Washers

Drips can be very annoying, not only because of the constant noise but because they cause stains on sanitary ware which can be impossible to remove if left for any length of time. It is not the most difficult job in the world to renew a tap washer though one might think so when one sees the number of houses which have dripping taps. In some areas local water authorities will replace tap washers free of charge, so it is worth ringing them first to find out. If not, then you will probably have to do it yourself. Most taps, whether in bath, basin or sink, need the same treatment, although bath taps usually have a larger washer.

Before beginning any work, always

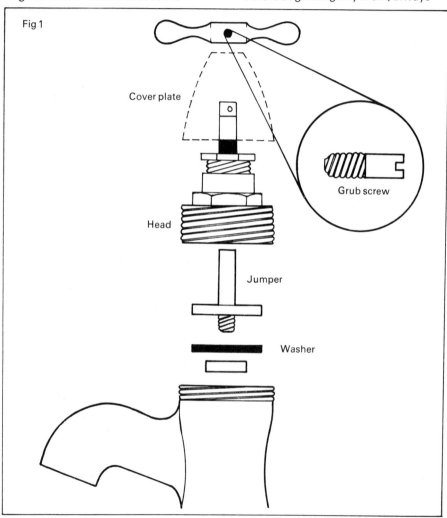

Fig 1

Cover plate

Grub screw

Head

Jumper

Washer

make sure that the water has been turned off (the cold supply stop tap is usually under the kitchen sink and the hot domestic supply in the airing cupboard). Once this has been done, turn on the taps to allow water which is still in the pipes to drain off. Open any other tap on the same supply— either hot or cold—to release air and allow the water to drain properly. Put in the plug firmly to avoid losing any

small parts down the waste pipe.

Find the grub screw that holds the turning part of the tap; this is usually in the side (Fig 1) or, on more modern taps, under a cover plate located on the top (Fig 2). Tap or prise the head off and unscrew the domed cover plate to expose the head. You may need a pair of pliers to remove the cover; if so place a piece of rag around it to protect the chrome. The handles of some taps now act as the cover for the head, so that once the handle is removed the head is exposed.

Using a spanner remove the head, which will expose the jumper and the washer. Pull out the jumper, unscrew the washer and replace it with a new one. Check that there is no grit on the seating in the tap bottom. Should the sealer be worn then a reseating tool is required. This can be hired or bought quite cheaply. Now put the whole assembly back together again and apply Vaseline to the threaded and moving parts.

Once this is done, turn off any taps you had opened before turning on the water supply again. Once the water is turned back on, open the taps to release any air from the pipes.

One sort of tap we have not dealt with yet is the super tap (Fig 3). It is not necessary to turn off the water when replacing a washer on this tap. Loosen the locking nut above the tap nozzle, and turn the tap on. Water will run out but gradually stop. Once the flow has stopped continue to unscrew, and when the nut is undone tap gently, and the washer, jumper and anti-splash device will be released. Renew the washer and reassemble.

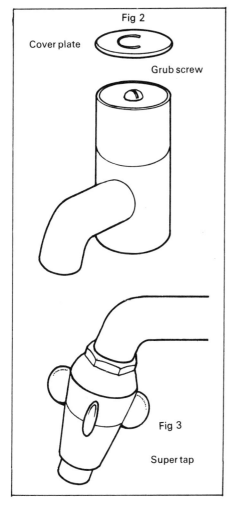

Fig 2

Cover plate

Grub screw

Fig 3

Super tap

Heating and Insulation

Thermostats

Setting water temperature and room temperature is usually done with thermostats. Their function is to switch on the boiler or immersion heater automatically when the temperature drops below the selected level.

If your hot water is heated by an immersion heater the thermostat will be found under the top cover. Before removing this cover turn off the electricity supply. Then undo the retaining screw to give access to the thermostat (Fig 1). You will see an arrow and calibrated lines with the temperature marked on them, either in centigrade or fahrenheit. Select the temperature required by turning the arrow with a small screwdriver. Then reassemble the cover plate and switch on the electricity.

Heating boilers will have a water temperature control on the boiler. The position and design of these vary according to the type of model but they all function in the same way. There will probably be a locking screw to be undone in order to alter the temperature of the water. After selecting the required temperature tighten the screw.

Room temperatures are selected either from one centrally sited thermostat, usually in the hall, or from individual thermostats in each room. When the temperature drops below the setting, the boiler will ignite to bring the temperature back up to the level required. The setting of wall thermostats is just as easy as any other type, by turning a knob to the desired

room temperature (Fig 2). Wall-mounted thermostats are connected by cables to the boiler so when the temperature drops a micro switch makes the contact to start the boiler or appliance connected to it. There are also types that fit directly to a radiator and when the air temperature drops below the setting they automatically open a valve and let hot water flow through to the radiator (Fig 3).

Maintenance

Central heating systems usually have the water circulated by a pump which frequently cannot be dismantled for maintenance. If a squeak does start in a central heating pump, then locate the central heating header water tank—which is usually in the loft space—remove the lid and give a squirt of washing-up liquid. Make sure not to overdo this—an egg-cupful should be adequate—and don't forget to replace the lid. Next you will have to drain off about two gallons of water from one of the downstairs radiators or any radiator that has a drain cock. This allows the liquid in the header tank to circulate into the heating system and as the liquid reaches the pump so the squeak will disappear. Do not forget to turn off the radiator drain cock after releasing the water.

Roof Insulation

By insulating the roof area not only will you save money over a period of time, but you will benefit by having a warmer house. There are several different types of insulating material. The most common are fibre-glass rolls that come in several different thicknesses—

25mm (1in), 50mm (2in) and 75mm (3in) being the most common (Fig 4). Remember the greater the thickness the better the insulation value.

The other common type of insulation is Vermiculite granules which come in large bags. To lay this you simply pour the granules from the bag and spread them between the joists, levelling off at the desired thickness with a shaped piece of wood (Fig 5). To lay the glass-fibre you need to roll the fibre between the joists. Use a pair of gloves for fibre-glass and tie them at the wrist to avoid any irritation to the skin.

Insulation of Pipes

Water pipes, both hot and cold, need to be insulated against freezing weather and heat loss. The most vulnerable place for pipes to freeze is in the roof area. It is false security to insulate a loft and not the surrounding pipes, since there is no warm air seeping through to keep water pipes from freezing.

There are several types of insulation for pipes. If the pipes are already fixed use either the bandage type (Fig 6) or the split tube (Fig 7). The bandage is made either from thick felt material or fibre-glass rolls, while the split tube will be either of foam or rubber. The foam lengths are easily slid on to the pipe and held in place by sticking the edges together or binding with wire or sellotape. Any outside pipes and even pipes running down the inside of garage walls need to be insulated. If you have an outside tap, you should not only insulate the pipe, but make a box to fit over the tap or the whole of the exposed pipe (Fig 8). Fill the inside with fibre-glass.

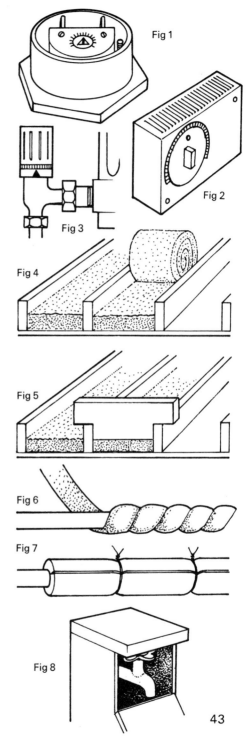

Fig 1

Fig 2

Fig 3

Fig 4

Fig 5

Fig 6

Fig 7

Fig 8

43

Repairing a Chair

A wobbly chair is neither the most comfortable thing to sit in, nor is it safe to use for standing on. Chairs are usually abused by people rocking back on them; this puts great stress and strain on the legs and joints, so that in time the glue holding the legs and rails may break, causing the chair to wobble. If left unchecked the chair will eventually fall apart, and it is obviously advisable to take steps to prevent this.

The chair must be taken apart before beginning any repairs; use a hammer and a block of wood to push out the joints (Fig 1). Number all the pieces as you take them off, as this will make reassembly much easier. Once the chair has been dismantled clean all traces of adhesive from the joints with a scraper or knife. Then reassemble the chair using your numbered guide, putting fresh wood glue on each joint as you do so. Tap each piece home using either a mallet or a hammer with a block of wood.

If any of the joints are loose they can be tightened in this way: cut a slot no deeper than the shoulder line (Fig 2); then cut a wedge 5mm ($\frac{1}{4}$in) shorter than the length of the saw cut. Apply adhesive to the two parts and start the wedges into the saw cut (Fig 3); then hammer home, making sure the expansion does not occur with the grain as this may split the wood (Fig 4).

If a rail has split, take it out and drill two screw holes on one side (Fig 5). Apply adhesive to the split edge and marry the two pieces together. Hold them together with a clamp or vice whilst you insert the screws, and once the screws are driven in wipe any surplus adhesive from the wood and leave to dry before assembling.

Fixing a Mirror

Fixing a mirror to a wall is not difficult as long as you follow a few simple rules. After deciding on its position, mark a line on the wall to indicate the position of the bottom of the mirror,

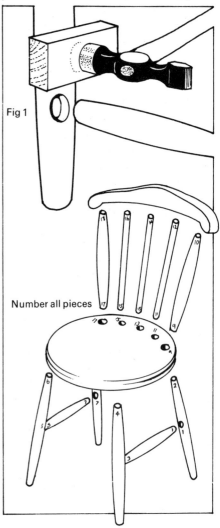

Fig 1

Number all pieces

making sure that it is level. Holding the mirror to the line, mark the position of the holes with a bradawl. Then remove the mirror to a safe place and drill the holes to the required depth (see Fixing into Masonry). Using domeheaded screws (see Screws) place these through the holes in the mirror, and put a rubber washer on to the screws, against the back of the mirror (see Fig 6).

Position the mirror and screws on the wall, locating the plastic wall plugs by turning the screws in by hand. When all the screws have been located, tighten them up with a screwdriver. The art of screwing mirrors to a wall is for the screws to just hold the glass firm ; tighten them too much and the mirror will break.

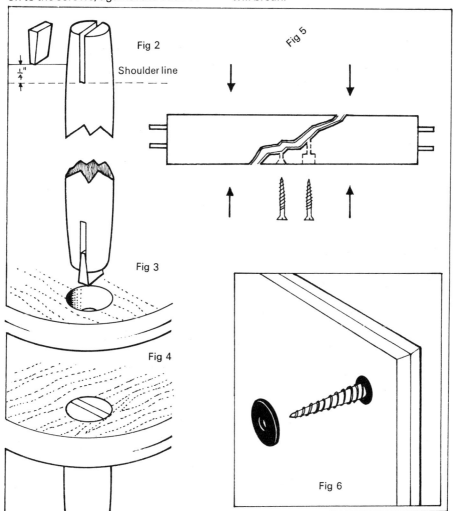

Fig 2

Shoulder line

$\frac{1}{4}"$

Fig 5

Fig 3

Fig 4

Fig 6

Woodworm and Household Pests

Every home opens its doors to visitors. Friends and relations come and go but there are also many visitors both welcome and unwelcome, who do not need to have the door opened to let them in. Wasps, moths, flies, ants, earwigs, silverfish, spiders, mice and bats are but a few of these. Most of the unpleasant ones can be removed by proprietary brands of sprays and baits but the most feared bug, grub or insect is probably the woodworm. Detected by the small round holes or fine powder which it leaves, this little grub will eat away timber at a frighteningly fast rate. Therefore, precautions must be taken as soon as you detect it.

If the wood affected is a piece of furniture then the cure is fairly simple. Take the offending piece of furniture out of doors and remove enough of the upholstery, drawers or doors to let you get at the affected area. It is fairly easy to treat this by painting the surface with a proprietary worm killer, applying several coats and letting the liquid soak into the wood ; alternatively, if there are only a few small holes, use a can with a thin spout to inject each hole. Several types of worm killer are available in cans with the necessary spout. You will find that as you squirt the fluid into one hole it will reappear from another, but make sure that each hole is treated separately.

Apart from liquids there are various types of worm killer and wood preservative in paste form. The paste is smeared onto the surface of the wood and then left to soak in. This may take several days, depending on the hardness of the wood. The advantage of paste is that it is easy to apply and the penetration is very good. Wood that has been treated with any worm killer should be left for several weeks before painting or polishing, and the worm holes should be filled before this is done. Keep a regular check to make sure that the grubs are dead ; should any new holes or dust appear the treatment must be undertaken again.

Unfortunately the roof area is a good target for woodworm so if you find that your loft or attic is infested you have a major problem. If the attack is not too severe then you may wish to tackle the job yourself. The loft must first be cleared of anything you may have stored there and boards laid out over the joists so that you can move around easily without putting your feet through the ceiling. Large affected areas are treated by sprays which can be hired from your local hire-shop.

You will need some protective clothing, the minimum being goggles and face mask. The spray canister is pumped up to the necessary pressure and then you should start at one end of the roof and work your way to the other end, making sure that you spray all the roof and ceiling timbers.

Important Points

Remember to keep the loft trapdoor shut ; beware of spraying near any electric lights and switches ; and make sure that you cover any water tanks in the roof area. If you feel there is extensive woodworm, call in experts on woodworm control as prolonged attacks will weaken the roof timbers and some rafters may have to be replaced.

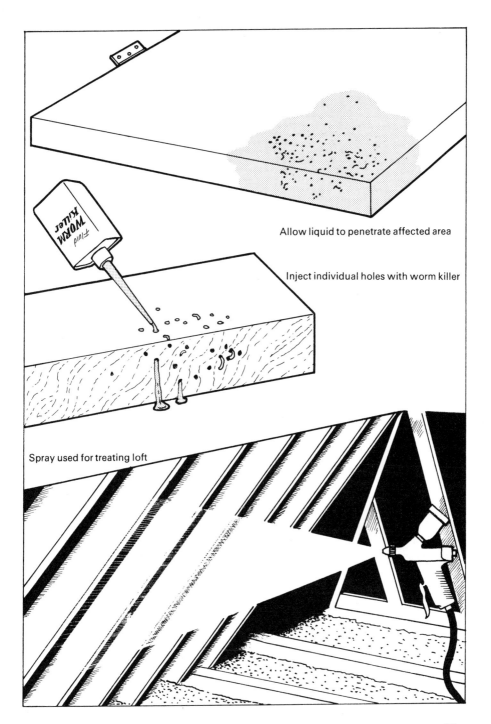

Allow liquid to penetrate affected area

Inject individual holes with worm killer

Spray used for treating loft

The Fireplace

Removing a Fireplace

In many older houses there is frequently an abundance of fireplaces, even in the bedrooms, and it is often an advantage to remove the fireplace to make room for fitted wardrobes ; or you may perhaps want to redesign a fireplace in the living area.

Whatever idea you have in mind, removing the existing fire surround is not a difficult job, but it is rather dirty, with the years of soot and debris which have accumulated in the chimney. Before you begin, clear the room of all furniture and seal any doors with sticky tape to stop the dust filtering through.

Most tiled fireplaces are held back to the wall with fixing lugs and these must be exposed. Chip away 25mm (1in) of plaster all around the fireplace ; this will stop any large lumps of plaster falling off as the fireplace is levered away from the wall, and also expose the fixing lugs. Remove the screws from the fixing lugs and then, using an iron bar, lever the fireplace away from the wall. When this has been removed, clear out all the fire back and rubble ; this may have to be broken up with a hammer and iron chisel. The hearth is usually bedded on a weak mortar mix and will lift off quite easily with the iron bar. After all the rubble has been cleared it is advisable to sweep the chimney to remove any accumulation of soot, if this has not already been done.

If the fireplace is to be boarded over then you will have to either cap off the chimney or fit a ventilator where the fireplace was. Capping the chimney is the better way as this will prevent rainwater from dropping down the chimney, but it does mean climbing up to the chimney to do the job.

Building a Fireplace

Should you decide to build your own fireplace you would be well advised to look at what some of the fireplace manufacturers are offering, because there are many kits available in stone, brick and slate. Many of these firms will build you a fireplace to your own design and measurements and will advise you if necessary on any problems that arise.

Fireplace kits generally come numbered and with full instructions so it really is quite simple, in fact, almost like painting by numbers. A word of warning !—a stone fireplace is very heavy, so if your design overhangs the width of the chimney breast then the floor beneath the stone work will need to be supported if it is a wooden suspended floor ; on solid concrete or asphalt floors, there is no such problem.

When selecting or designing your fireplace remember you could incorporate a shelf for the television, stereo, aquarium or even a small cupboard, and the fireplace can thus become a main feature of the house.

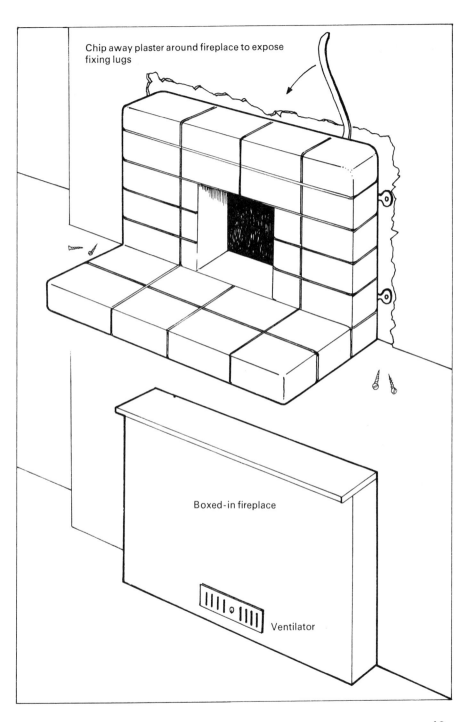

Chip away plaster around fireplace to expose fixing lugs

Boxed-in fireplace

Ventilator

Replacing a Tile

Cracked, chipped or broken tiles are both unsightly and unhygienic, and it is quite easy to replace them when you know how. First you must remove any grout from around the edges of the tile, using an old kitchen knife, to clean all debris from around the edges. Then use a small iron chisel to break the tile from the centre outwards. Do not try to lever the tile from the edges, as this will only break the surrounding tiles, but chip out small pieces at a time.

When all the tile has been removed, clean off any adhesive remaining on the wall and make sure there are no bumps or high spots. If you don't get rid of these, the new tile will not bed in level with the existing tiles. Make sure the replacement tile fits into the opening, and if it is a fraction too large,

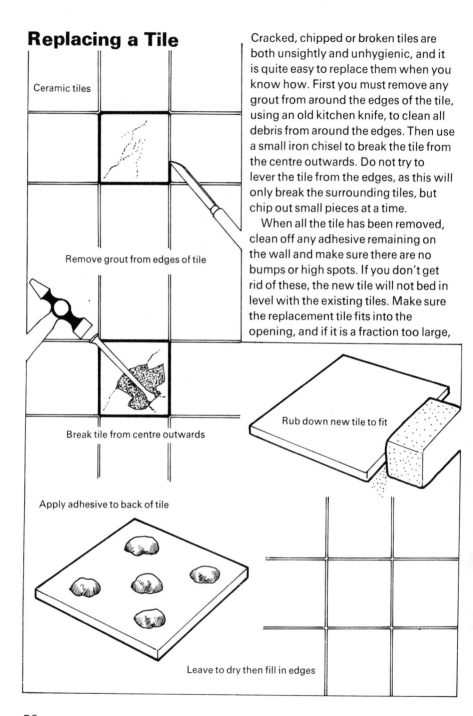

Ceramic tiles

Remove grout from edges of tile

Break tile from centre outwards

Rub down new tile to fit

Apply adhesive to back of tile

Leave to dry then fill in edges

rub down the edges on a piece of yorkstone or something similar. Once it fits, apply the correct adhesive to the back of the tile and push into position so that it is flush with the surrounding tiles. Leave it to dry for four to five hours, and once it is set fill in the edges with grouting powder mixed with water.

One problem when repairing tiles in this way is that the replacement may be a different shade from the others, so when you are putting up tiles in a kitchen or bathroom always keep a few spare for such emergencies, then if you have to replace a tile at any time you can be sure that the colour will be exactly the same.

A similar procedure is followed for replacing a lino tile which has worn

badly. Once again, remember not to damage the edges of the surrounding floor tiles, and prise the tile up with an old kitchen knife. If the tile is difficult to lift then apply heat with a fan heater onto its surface. This will soften the adhesive enough to make its removal easier. Once all the pieces of tile are removed scrape the adhesive from the floor, making absolutely sure there are no high points as these will show through the new tile once it is laid. Trim the new tile to fit with a Stanley knife and spread onto the floor. Then press down the tile, working from one side towards the other so as not to trap any air. Remove any of the adhesive which has squeezed through and try not to walk on the tile until the adhesive has dried.

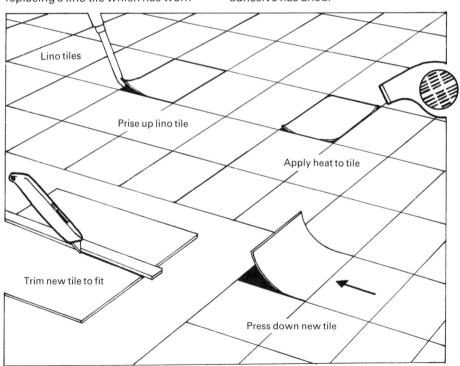

Lino tiles

Prise up lino tile

Apply heat to tile

Trim new tile to fit

Press down new tile

51

Floor Levelling

Wood Floors

If you are about to lay lino, cork or vinyl tiles onto a wood floor the surface must be even and level otherwise any defects will show through, such as warped floorboards, or nails that have risen above the boards due to wear. Therefore the floor should be levelled. Any protruding nails need to be punched below the surface, then the floorboards need to be sanded level using a large floor sander available on hire from most good hire shops. Only when the floor is absolutely level and flat should tiles be laid. Any wide joints between the floorboards should also be filled with papier mâché and sanded flat and dry. It is as well to remember when using a professional sander to sand across the boards at an angle of 45° to the grain (Fig 1) otherwise, if used at right angles to the boards, the sander will merely ride over the bumps.

An alternative method of levelling a wood floor is to lay sheets of hardboard and nail these to the floorboards.

Fig 1 Sand floor at 45° angle to grain of floorboards

Stagger the joints (Fig 2) between the sheets and nail down. Starting from the centre of the sheet nail at 200mm (8in) intervals and 100mm (4in) intervals around the edges.

Cement or Tiled Floors

Cement or tiled floors are perhaps more difficult to level as you cannot nail hardboard to them; consequently different techniques have to be used. First you must inspect the floor for any sign of damp—if you lay tiles onto a damp floor the tiles will eventually lift. A simple check is to warm a piece of flat metal on a cooker or with a blowlamp. When warm, place the metal onto the floor and leave until it cools. If the floor is damp the piece of metal will have beads of moisture underneath it and there will be a damp patch on the floor. Use this method on several parts of the floor to ascertain the extent of damp area.

There are several ways to tackle this kind of damp; one of the most successful is to apply two coats of Synthaprufe. This should be applied also to the wall up to the damp course. When the Synthaprufe has dried apply a proprietary floor-levelling compound such as Arduit Z8 or F9. These compounds are self-levelling so very little trowel work is required. The Arduite F9 when mixed with the correct amount of water can be spread with a soft broom and left to level itself; as these materials harden they provide a very smooth and level surface. Non-porous floors, ie quarry tiles, that need to be levelled will require Ardex neoprene primer before applying the levelling compounds.

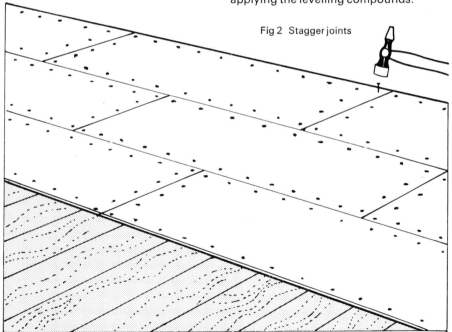

Fig 2 Stagger joints

Laying Floor Tiles

If you are about to lay floor tiles it is necessary to spend some time considering where to start. Against the longest wall seems the most obvious place to begin but do not be misguided. Buildings are very rarely square, so if you use this as a starting point invariably the tiles will run out of true line. Always stack the tiles loosely in a warm room for a day or so before you start work. This will make the tiles more supple and easier to work with.

So where do you start? First lay out some tiles on the floor; butt the edges together and mark each joint onto a rod, eg a piece of lath. This will act as a guide when setting out the floor. Using the rod as a guide, mark a line near the centre of the room. Allowance must be made for trimming the edge tiles. Check the other side of the room with the rod to make sure that you avoid having to cut a narrow strip of tile that is not only unsightly but difficult to fix. When the best starting position is found mark both ends of the room and join marks with a tape or chalk line. Do exactly the same for the other two walls. Where the two lines cross will be the starting points.

Some tiles are self-adhesive and need only the paper backs removed before sticking down. If your tiles need adhesive then spread about 1 sq m (about 1 sq yd) of adhesive at a time, being careful not to obscure the chalk lines. Place the first tile true to the chalk lines, then proceed to lay the other tiles, taking care not to squeeze any adhesive onto the face of the tiles.

Do not slide the tiles into place as this will squeeze the adhesive out of the joints. They need to be placed down so that the two edges butt up against the last tile. Roll down any edges that are not flat with a small wooden roller. Any adhesive on the face of the tile should be removed immediately, following the manufacturer's instructions as to what solvent should be used.

After sticking down the first square metre, apply the adhesive to the next area and so on until you are two tiles from the edge of the walls. It is better now to allow the area just laid time to dry as cutting in the tiles around the edge calls for working on the tiles so there is a chance that you may move them by working on the tiles whilst still wet. Also make sure that all excess adhesive is cleared from the finishing edge of the tiles otherwise, when you come to lay the last two tiles, you will be unable to press them level because of the hardened adhesive.

When the tiles have dried sufficiently to work on you can proceed to fill in the margin. This is done by butting one tile against the last centre one laid. Lay another tile on top, but this one should be butted against the skirting board. With a Stanley knife score the tile underneath, break the tile on this line and trim the edge clean. Place the cut tile and the full tile into position, remembering to put the cut edge to the skirting. The two tiles should now fit like a glove. Continue fitting the tiles into the margin in this manner. When cutting the tile to fit around a doorway the tile should finish half-way under the door when the door is closed.

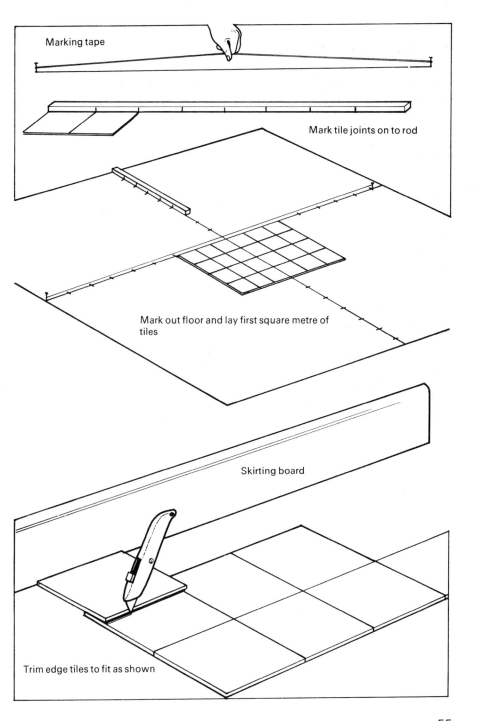

Marking tape

Mark tile joints on to rod

Mark out floor and lay first square metre of tiles

Skirting board

Trim edge tiles to fit as shown

55

Cement and Sand

Cement and sand are part of the heavy brigade in home maintenance; nevertheless these materials will be needed for certain maintenance jobs in and around the home. There are several useful tips about using cement that will make life that much easier. First of all, let us look at the materials themselves.

Cement

This comes in 50kg (one hundred-weight) bags which are very heavy, so if you need only small amounts try to buy a split bag; this may be messy but it is cheaper. Most builders' merchants have a split bag or a bin in which the cement is kept and sold in small lots. There are also several different types of cement—some for brickwork, some for concrete, fast-setting and of course coloured.

Sand

This also comes in different grades, soft for brickwork and plaster and rough for floors. This latter should always be used for floors as it gives strength to the cement so that the floor does not wear and cause the surface to dust up.

Mixing the cement and sand together is a job that must be done thoroughly. Turn the required mix over three times dry and three times wet to ensure they are completely mixed. Quantities of sand and cement vary according to what you are using them for. Three parts sand to one part cement is a good guide if mixing by hand, but if you are using a cement mixer four parts sand and one part cement will be just as strong since the cement mixer will blend the sand and cement quicker and more efficiently than by hand.

Water content is also important,

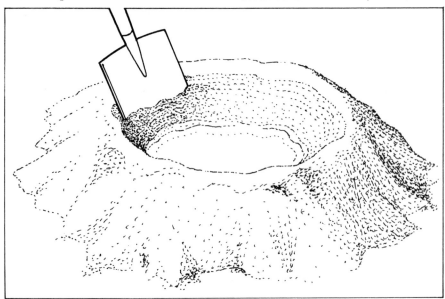

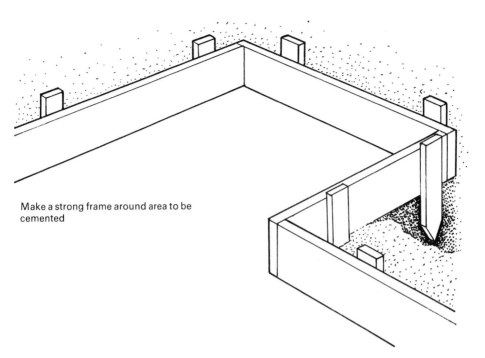

Make a strong frame around area to be cemented

since the mix needs to be of a good, thick, creamy consistency when you are laying bricks. One way of achieving this is to add washing-up liquid to a mix to make the sand and cement creamy and easier to work. A thimbleful for every gallon of water is adequate. If you are using sand and cement for a floor, the mix should be nearly dry. When you pick up a handful of the mix, it should just hold together if it is the right consistency. If the mix is too wet the cement will float to the top as you are trowelling the floor, and this will cause weak mix under the surface and the floor may eventually break up.

Cement and sand for small jobs around the house can be bought in pre-mixed bags containing the correct amount of sand and cement in grades for bricks, plaster, floors, etc.

Ready-mixed Concrete

Another source of supply for cement and sand is to buy ready-mixed concrete, which can be delivered to your home. The dealer will insist on a minimum delivery of cubic metres, so check this first with your local supplier whose address can be found in the yellow pages. Check also that the delivery lorry has access to your property. Ready-mixed concrete has a lot of advantages over mixing concrete by hand and you can be sure that the mixture is of the correct consistency. There is, as in all good things, one problem and that is that ready-mixed concrete sets in about one hour, depending on the weather, so do have at hand a willing band of helpers with shovels to help you spread it.

Pointing Brickwork

Repointing brickwork is almost certainly the most laborious job in house maintenance. Of course, not every house needs to be repointed, but it is very often necessary on older properties, and Building Societies, when they offer a mortgage, often stipulate that certain areas of the brickwork must be repointed. These are often the walls most exposed to extremes of weather, and the worst of all is frequently the chimney, probably the most exposed of all the brickwork. It is common to find the cement falling out of the brick joints here and if not attended to the chimney will eventually fall down. If your chimney does need repointing you will need some form of scaffolding to do the job safely. This can be hired, but you may feel that this job needs professionals, as not everyone likes venturing out onto a roof.

If the area to be repointed is fairly large then do hire a tower frame, as this will make working much easier and safer (Fig 1). Tools which you will need are shown in Fig 2. The first job is to rake out all the loose mortar, working on 1 square metre (approx 10 sq ft) at a time. Use an iron chisel and cut out the old mortar to a depth of 15mm ($\frac{1}{2}$in). Clean out the vertical joints first, then the horizontal ones, and use the head of a soft brush to remove any cement dust from the joints. When 1 sq m (approx 10 sq ft) has been finished, start the next but remember never to reach out too far from the scaffolding. When the whole wall has been cut out and brushed down, clean away all the old debris and place a board against the bottom of the wall. This will catch any cement droppings and thus avoid making any marks and stains on paving slabs or paths. When mixing the new mortar you should try to get the mixture as near as possible in texture to the old. This, of course, is difficult to tell precisely, so as a guide, mix one measure of lime, and one of cement to five of soft sand. Do not mix up too much at a time and don't forget to add a small squeeze of washing-up liquid.

The procedure for pointing is to fill the vertical joints first then the horizontal. There are several ways of filling the joints, and you will find which suits you best. You can either load the hawk and then scoop a small amount along the trowel and push it into the joints (Fig 3) or use a piece of hose-pipe, and do the same, rubbing well into the joints (Fig 4). Another method is to hold the hawk against the lower edge of the joint and push the mortar off it into the cracks (Fig 5).

After the mortar has set, rub the joints with a piece of bent round iron or a piece of hose-pipe so as to indent the mortar, and finally brush off any waste from the joints and brickwork with a soft broom. Before you start repointing a wall you should dampen it by flicking water onto the brickwork and joints with an old brush. This is to prevent the brickwork absorbing the moisture from the new mortar.

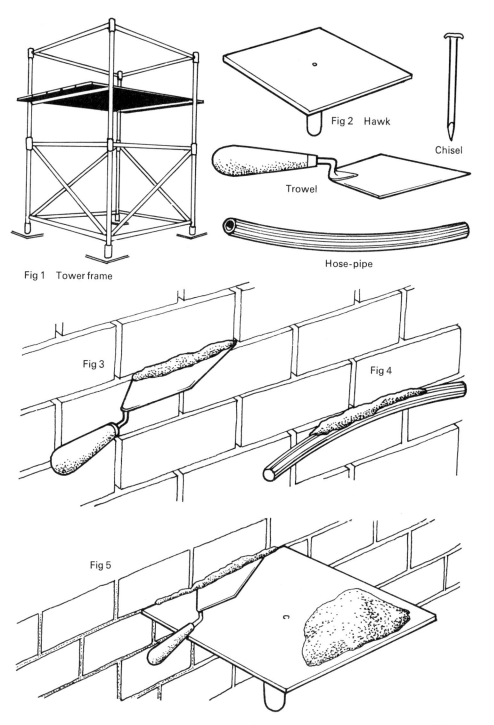

Fig 1   Tower frame

Fig 2   Hawk

Chisel

Trowel

Hose-pipe

Fig 3

Fig 4

Fig 5

Gutters

Dripping gutters are one of the big nuisances about the home. Have you noticed how they can wash away the earth from plants, and cause rust marks on paving slabs? To make any repairs to gutters or drain pipes you will obviously need a ladder. If you don't own one, they are inexpensive to hire. When working on a gutter you will find that a 'stand off' will be a great asset (Fig 1). This device will keep the ladder away from the gutter, making the work involved easier and much safer. It is also very simple to fit as it hooks over two of the rungs of the ladder and is held in place by a spring hook attached to the rung below.

Gutters made of iron will tend to rust over the years, especially where there is no paint, and often at the back where they are attached to the facia. Joints that are made with red lead tend to harden and allow water to seep through. To replace a section of worn guttering, undo the two nuts that hold the joints together. If they are rusted in cut them off with a small hacksaw. Then tap the joints apart with a hammer, taking care not to break the guttering. Lift the worn section out and lower it to the ground. The two remaining ends of the gutter should then be cleaned with a wire brush, and all moisture dried from them. The new piece of gutter should be painted at the back with Bitumastic paint to protect the area where, when the gutter is fixed, you are unable to paint. When joining the two ends it is sensible to use a waterproof sealant. Apply this to the overlapping ends of the two sections and bolt them together using 6 × 25mm ($\frac{1}{4}$ × 1in) bolts. As these are tightened up so the sealant makes a waterproof joint. Paint the inside of the gutter with Bitumastic paint, and the outside to match the existing paintwork.

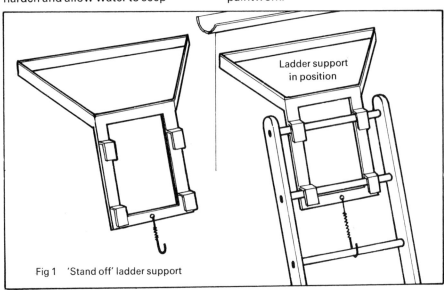

Ladder support in position

Fig 1 'Stand off' ladder support

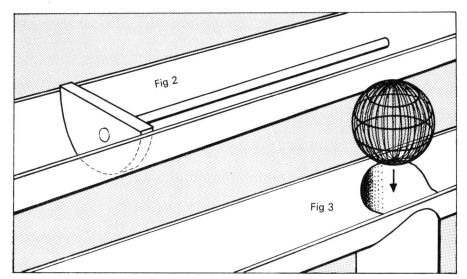

Fig 2

Fig 3

Down pipes usually suffer at the back because you cannot reach them with a paint brush. If they have rusted through they will also have to be renewed, so start at the top by removing the screws and lowering the whole pipe. Replacing it is just as easy since there are no joints to make. Simply place one end into the socket and fix it back to the wall, remembering to paint with Bitumastic in the inaccessible side. If trees overhang your house you will have to clear any leaves and debris from the gutters every year. A scraper (Fig 2) will make this job simpler and easier, but remember never to over-reach when standing on a ladder.

It is a good idea to place a galvanized wire balloon into the drainpipe outlet to stop the leaves blocking it (Fig 3). If you have a lot of guttering to be renewed, you would be well advised to think of replacing it with the plastic type since this needs no maintenance or painting, except for cleaning and the occasional wash with soapy water.

Ladders and Safety

Whether you own your own ladder or hire one the procedures to be followed for safety on ladders are the same. Too many people fall off ladders, so do take care. Never over-reach from a ladder— you should come down and move the ladder along. Always place the ladder on firm even ground and never wedge the ladder on bricks or similar objects. The safest method is to always have someone standing on the bottom to stop the ladder sliding.

Use good footwear on ladders— soft-soled shoes like plimsolls will make your feet tire very quickly, so wear a pair of hard-soled shoes. Also, tuck your trousers into your socks ; this will prevent you from treading on the bottom of your trousers as you climb or descend the ladder.

Never leave a ladder lying around ; always hang it away and padlock it safely, as a ladder is an ideal piece of equipment for any would-be burglar.

Fences

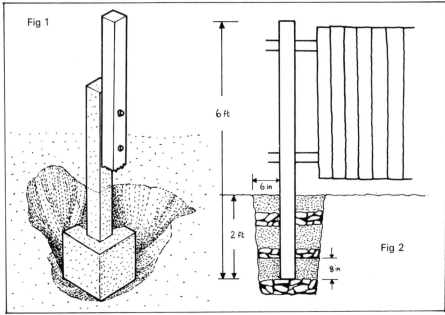

Fig 1

6 ft

6 in

2 ft

8 in

Fig 2

Fences seem always to be falling over and their slats or boards falling off. The main problem is usually that the wooden posts tend to rot through ; this need not happen if they have been treated correctly at the beginning, but this is often neglected.

If you do find that you need to replace rotten posts, the whole section of fence will have to be taken down in order to give access to them, so that stumps can be dug out. The best method for replacing the posts is to substitute the bottom half with a concrete spur (Fig 1) ; this should be driven into the ground and then either set into concrete or have the earth rammed in hard around it. The broken upper part of the wooden post can then be used by bolting it to the concrete spur, after first trimming off any rotten wood, and then dipping the

post in creosote. The fence is then rebuilt on the posts. The advantage of this method is that it will outlast any wooden post set into the ground.

If you are replacing with wood then place it in an old bath or some similar large receptacle and soak the bottom half of each post in creosote or any other wood preservative. You can buy timber already preserved at most good timber merchants.

After the posts have been soaked in preservative dig a hole : do not dig the hole too big. Allow 150mm (6in) on all sides of the post. A 2m (6ft) post should be sunk into the ground to a depth of 600mm (2ft). Drop in some small rubble and flatten this down firmly with a length of wood. Place the post into the hole and ram in 200mm (8in) of earth until the post is held firmly. Continue in this manner until the hole is filled, checking at each stage that the post is upright (Fig 2).

If the posts are to support a very heavy fence in an exposed position then you will be advised to use concrete instead of earth. Ram earth down the first 200mm (8in) of the post; this will support the post in an upright position while you pour in the concrete. Always finish the concrete 100mm (4in) below the ground level so that earth may be filled in the top and do check that the post is upright before the concrete sets. If you are completely renewing your fencing, then it is always better to use concrete posts. I agree they are not so good to look at and easy to handle but their life is far longer than wood.

The cladding of fences can be made of many different sorts of wood, but one problem is that after several years the slats tend to come loose. It is a simple job to nail back the boards that have become loose, but you should make sure the bottoms do not touch the ground as this will draw up moisture from the earth and in time will rot the boards. If this has happened then you should cut the bottom off about 150mm (6in) above the ground and replace it with a gravel board (Fig 3). One way of getting a nice straight line to cut along, is to use a string covered with chalk (Fig 4). One final thing to remember about fences is to give them a coat of creosote every now and then to prevent decay.

Fig 3

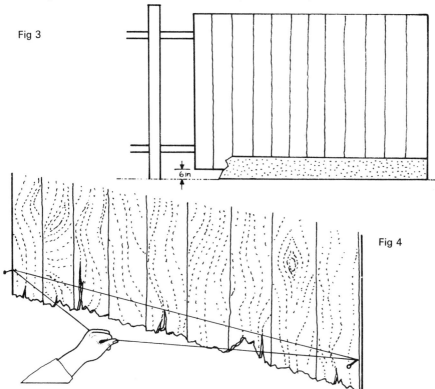

6in

Fig 4

Bibliography

Alexander, J. *Home Decoration* (Pelham Books, 1970)
Bowyer, J. *Central Heating* (David & Charles, 1977)
Day, Roy. *All About House Repair and Maintenance* (Hamlyn, 1976)
——, ——. *All About Plumbing and Central Heating* (Hamlyn, 1976)
Hall, E. and Wilkins, Tony. *Home Plumbing* (Newnes-Butterworth, 1977)
Johnson, David. *Home Improvements: A DIY Guide* (Stanley Paul, 1973)
——, ——. *Home Decorating* (Penny Pincher) (David & Charles, 1979)
McLaughlin, T. *Make Your Own Electricity* (David & Charles, 1977)
Reader's Digest. *Home Decorating* (Reader's Digest, 1976)
Richardson, S. A. *Protecting Buildings* (David & Charles, 1977)
Swindells, Tony. 1001 *Ways of Saving Money* (David & Charles, 1978)
Taylor, Alan. *Home Maintenance and Repairs* (MacGibbon and Kee, 1972)
——, ——. *Do-it-yourself Home Improvements* (Hart-Davis, 1975)

Magazines

Homemaker, King's Reach Tower, Stamford Street, London SE1 9LS
Do it Yourself, Link House, Dingwall Avenue, Croydon, Surrey CR9 2TA

British Library Cataloguing in Publication Data

Smith, Michael
    Everyday home repairs – (Penny pinchers)
    1. Dwellings – Maintenance and repair –
    Amateurs manuals
    I. Title   II. Series
    643'.7   TH4817.3
    ISBN 0-7153-7553-9

Typeset and printed in Great Britain
by Redwood Burn Limited Trowbridge
for David & Charles (Publishers) Limited
Brunel House   Newton Abbot   Devon

Published in the United States of America
by David & Charles Inc
North Pomfret   Vermont 05053   USA